Study Guide
Practice Workbook

Mathematics
Applications and Connections

Course 3

Glencoe
McGraw-Hill

New York, New York   Columbus, Ohio   Woodland Hills, California   Peoria, Illinois

To the Student

This *Study Guide and Practice Workbook* gives you additional examples and practice for the concept exercises in each lesson. The exercises are designed to aid your study of mathematics by reinforcing important mathematical skills needed to succeed in the everyday world. The material is organized by chapter and lesson, with one study guide worksheet and one practice worksheet for every lesson in *Mathematics: Applications and Connections,* Course 3.

Always keep your workbook handy. Along with your textbook, daily homework, and class notes, the completed *Study Guide and Practice Workbook* can help you in reviewing for quizzes and tests.

To the Teacher

Answers to each worksheet are found in the *Study Guide Masters* or *Practice Masters* booklets and also in the Teacher's Wraparound Edition of *Mathematics: Applications and Connections,* Course 3.

Glencoe/McGraw-Hill

A Division of The McGraw-Hill Companies

Send all inquiries to:
Glencoe/McGraw-Hill
8787 Orion Place
Columbus, OH 43240-4027

ISBN: 0-02-833125-7   *Study Guide and Practice Workbook,* Course 3

17 18 19 20 21 024   08 07 06 05

Contents

1-1 **Study Guide**

A Plan for Problem Solving

Angela sold a computer for $2,029.80 and a printer for $895.95. If the total amount paid was $3,121.70, how much was the sales tax?

Explore	What do you know? the sale = $2,029.80 + $895.95 total paid = $3,121.70 What are you trying to find? the amount of the sales tax
Plan	Find the total sale amount. Subtract the total from $3,121.70. Estimate the answer. $2,000 + $900 = $2,900 $3,100 − $2,900 = $200 The tax was about $200.
Solve	total sale = $2,029.80 + $895.95 or $2,925.75 tax = $3,121.70 − $2,925.75 or $195.95
Examine	The answer is close to the estimate. The answer makes sense.

Use the four-step plan to solve each problem.

1. Suppose you are taking a 10 A.M. flight. It takes you 1 hour and 15 minutes to get up and ready to leave and 35 minutes to drive to the airport. If you want to be at the airport 1 hour before take-off, what time should you get up?

2. Leslie bought a shirt priced at $18.79 and a pair of socks priced at $4.69. What is the cost of the two items? How much change will he get from $25.00?

3. Tickets for the Pep Club barbecue were $8.00 for adults and $4.50 for students. If 68 adult tickets and 122 student tickets were sold, how much money did the Pep Club take in? How much did the Pep Club earn if barbecue expenses were $488?

4. Suppose you have 100 sugar cubes. How can you arrange the cubes in a rectangle so the fewest cubes will be on an outside edge? How can you arrange the sugar cubes in a rectangle so all of the cubes will be on an up side edge?

Name _____ **Date** _____

1-1 Practice

A Plan for Problem Solving

Use the four-step plan to solve each equation.

1. Geraldo has dowel pieces measuring 10 inches and 11 inches long. He places a number of the pieces end-to-end. They form a line 76 inches long. How many pieces of each size dowel does he have?

2. Jan's office contains 12 file cabinets. Three cabinets have 4 drawers, all the other cabinets have 5 drawers. Jane is typing new labels for each file cabinet drawer. How many labels will she need?

3. Bob has a stack of $1 bills, Ian has some $5 bills, and Kim has more than one $10 bill. Each person has the same amount of money. What is the least amount each one has?

4. Angeliki is sticking adhesive digits on the faces of some cuckoo clocks. She has separate compartments of 0s, 1s, 2s, and so on. If she completes 7 clock faces, how many individual digits does she use?

5. Joni walks once around the edge of the swimming pool. The rectangular-shaped pool is 60 feet long. If Joni walks a total of 176 feet, how wide is the pool?

6. The Elm Street bus passes Jamie's house every 20 minutes, and the Park bus passes every half hour. Both buses pass the house together at 1:10 P.M. When is the next time the buses pass together?

7. Jake is thinking of a number which, when multiplied times itself gives a product of 729. What is Jake's number?

8. Eric uses molten pewter to make dragon-shaped keychain ornaments. Each dragon weighs 2 ounces. How many dragons can Eric make if he uses 1.5 pounds of molten pewter? (16 ounces = 1 pound)

9. Ken is replacing the ceiling tiles in the school hallway. The hallway is 60 feet long and 8 feet wide. Each ceiling tile is 4 feet long and 2 feet wide. How many tiles does Ken need to complete the job?

10. Helene is recording a practice tape for her dance students. She will include rumbas, waltzes and one samba. Each rumba is 3 minutes long; each waltz, 4 minutes; and the samba, 2 minutes long. The tape will contain 30 minutes of music. If Helene wants to record at least 2 waltzes, how many songs of each type will she include in the collection?

1-2 Study Guide

Powers and Exponents

A **power** can be used to show a number multiplied by itself.

$3 \times 3 \times 3 \times 3$ can be written 3^4. It is read, "3 to the fourth power."

The *exponent,* 4, tells you how many times
the *base,* 3, is used as a factor.

base $\longrightarrow 3^4 \longleftarrow$ exponent

Example 1   Write $2 \cdot 2 \cdot 3 \cdot 2 \cdot 2 \cdot 3$ using exponents.

There are four factors of 2 and two factors of 3.
$2 \cdot 2 \cdot 3 \cdot 2 \cdot 2 \cdot 3 = 2^4 \cdot 3^2$

Multiply to find the value of expressions with exponents.

Examples   **2** Evaluate 3^4.

$3^4 = 3 \cdot 3 \cdot 3 \cdot 3$
$\quad = 81$

3 Evaluate $2^4 \cdot 3^2$.

$2^4 \cdot 3^2 = 2 \cdot 2 \cdot 2 \cdot 2 \cdot 3 \cdot 3$
$\qquad = 16 \cdot 9$
$\qquad = 144$

Write each expression using exponents.

1. $7 \cdot 7 \cdot 7 \cdot 6 \cdot 6 \cdot 6 \cdot 6$

2. $2 \cdot 2 \cdot 5 \cdot 5 \cdot 9 \cdot 9$

3. $10 \cdot 10 \cdot 8 \cdot 8$

Evaluate each expression.

4. 10^5

5. 2^5

6. 7^2

7. $3^3 \cdot 4^2$

8. $1^9 \cdot 5^3$

9. $100^2 \cdot 6^2$

10. 12^2

11. $2^4 \cdot 1^6$

12. 50^3

13. $7^2 \cdot 7^2$

14. $4^2 \cdot 3^2 \cdot 2^2$

15. $9^1 \cdot 9^2$

1-2 Practice

Powers and Exponents

Write each expression using exponents.

1. $4 \cdot 4$

2. $5 \cdot 5 \cdot 5 \cdot 5 \cdot 5 \cdot 5$

3. $2 \cdot 2 \cdot 2 \cdot 2 \cdot 2 \cdot 2 \cdot 2 \cdot 2$

4. $3 \cdot 3 \cdot 3$

5. $6 \cdot 6 \cdot 6 \cdot 6$

6. $7 \cdot 7 \cdot 7 \cdot 7 \cdot 7 \cdot 7 \cdot 7$

7. $9 \cdot 9 \cdot 9 \cdot 9 \cdot 9$

8. $4 \cdot 4 \cdot 4 \cdot 4$

Evaluate each expression.

9. 3^2

10. 2^5

11. 5^2

12. 5^3

13. 4^3

14. 2^3

Write each expression using exponents.

15. $2 \cdot 3 \cdot 2 \cdot 3 \cdot 2$

16. $3 \cdot 5 \cdot 5 \cdot 3$

17. $5 \cdot 7 \cdot 7 \cdot 7 \cdot 5 \cdot 5$

18. $2 \cdot 2 \cdot 2 \cdot 3 \cdot 2 \cdot 2$

19. $2 \cdot 3 \cdot 5 \cdot 2 \cdot 5 \cdot 2$

20. $2 \cdot 3 \cdot 2 \cdot 5 \cdot 2 \cdot 3 \cdot 2$

21. $2 \cdot 2 \cdot 3 \cdot 2 \cdot 5$

22. $5 \cdot 7 \cdot 2 \cdot 7 \cdot 5$

Evaluate each expression.

23. $2^2 \cdot 3^2$

24. $2^2 \cdot 11^3$

25. $2 \cdot 5 \cdot 7^2$

26. $3^3 \cdot 5^2$

27. $2^2 \cdot 3^3$

28. $2^3 \cdot 5^2 \cdot 7^1$

29. $2^3 \cdot 3^2$

30. $5^2 \cdot 7^3$

31. $3^3 - 2^2$

32. $1^3 + 1^4 + 1^5$

33. $2^4 + 3^5$

34. $2^2 \cdot 3^3 + 2^3 \cdot 3^2$

35. $2^5 + 5^2$

36. $3^4 \cdot 5^2 + 2^3 \cdot 3^2$

1-3 Study Guide

Variables, Expressions, and Equations

Letters called **variables** represent unknown quantities.
Expressions are algebraic phrases that contain variables.

Follow the order of
operations to evaluate
or find the value of an
expression.

Order of Operations
1. Do all operations within grouping symbols first; start with the innermost grouping symbols.
2. Do all powers before other operations.
3. Multiply and divide in order from left to right.
4. Add and subtract in order from left to right.

Examples **1** Evaluate $[5 + (6 - 4)^2] \div 3$.

$$[5 + (6 - 4)^2] \div 3 = (5 + 2^2) \div 3$$
$$= (5 + 4) \div 3$$
$$= 9 \div 3 \text{ or } 3$$

2 Evaluate $2a + bc$ if $a = 5$, $b = 3$, and $c = 10$.

$$2a + bc = 2(5) + 3(10)$$
$$= 10 + 30$$
$$= 40$$

A mathematical sentence that contains an "=" is called an **equation.**

Example 3   Find the solution set of $17n = 510$ if the value of n can be selected from the set $\{28, 30, 32\}$.

Try 28.
$$17n = 510$$
$$17(28) \stackrel{?}{=} 510$$
$$476 = 510 \quad \textit{False}$$

Try 30.
$$17n = 510$$
$$17(30) \stackrel{?}{=} 510$$
$$510 = 510 \quad \textit{True}$$

Try 32.
$$17n = 510$$
$$17(32) \stackrel{?}{=} 510$$
$$544 = 510 \quad \textit{False}$$

Evaluate each expression.

1. $(4^2 + 4) \div 4$

2. $56 \div [(5 - 3) \times 4]$

3. $5^2 \times 4 \div 10$

4. $15 - 2 \times 4 - (6 - 3)$

5. $[1 + (5 - 2)^2] \times 6$

6. $(4 \times 5)^2$

Evaluate each expression if $m = 4$, $n = 3$, and $p = 2$.

7. $7m - 3p$

8. $mn - p$

9. $2p + p^2$

10. $5m - 4n + p$

11. $(m - p)n$

12. $5p + m$

Find the solution for each equation from the given replacement set.

13. $k + 23 = 45$, $\{21, 22, 23\}$

14. $55 - d = 17$, $\{36, 37, 38\}$

15. $2p = \$19.80$, $\{\$9.00, \$9.45, \$9.90\}$

16. $\frac{p}{33} = 15$, $\{485, 495, 505\}$

Mathematics: Applications and Connections, Course 3

1-3 Practice

Variables, Expressions, and Equations

Evaluate each expression.

1. $30 - 2 \cdot 3$

2. $(6 - 4)^2$

3. $3(4) + 4(5)$

4. $(3 + 2^2) \cdot 2$

5. $[(6 + 3)5] \div 3$

6. $50 + 2[(8 - 3)2]$

7. $[10 - (9 - 6)^2] - 1$

8. $\frac{3 \cdot 2 + 6}{4} + 2(18 - 3)$

9. $\frac{60 - 4^2}{4} + 2 \cdot 4$

Evaluate each expression if $a = 5$, $b = 6$, $c = 4$, and $d = 3$.

10. abc^2

11. $3a - 3b$

12. $2ab + cd$

13. $10b - c - d$

14. $5a + 6b - c$

15. $(6a \div 2)d$

16. $2(ab + c) + d$

17. $10b \div c + b$

18. $(3a + 2c) \cdot dc$

Find the solution for each equation from the given replacement set.

19. $y - 13 = 18$, $\{21, 31, 41, 51\}$

20. $324 \div x = 36$, $\{6, 7, 8, 9\}$

21. $4z = 48$, $\{8, 10, 12, 14\}$

22. $630 - d = 546$, $\{64, 74, 84, 94\}$

23. $15 + x = 37$, $\{12, 22, 32, 42\}$

24. $a \div 13 = 9$, $\{97, 107, 117, 127\}$

25. $y + 45 = 80$, $\{25, 30, 35, 40\}$

26. $125 = 5x$, $\{15, 25, 35, 45\}$

1-4 Study Guide

Solving Subtraction and Addition Equations

If you add the same number to each side of an equation, the two sides remain equal.

Example 1 Solve $v - 65 = 21$. Check your solution.

$$v - 65 + 65 = 21 + 65 \qquad \text{Add 65 to each side of the equation.}$$
$$v = 86$$

Check: $v - 65 = 21$
$$86 - 65 \overset{?}{=} 21 \qquad \text{Replace } v \text{ with 86.}$$
$$21 = 21 \ ✔$$

If you subtract the same number from each side of an equation, the two sides remain equal.

Example 2 Solve $c + 34 = 99$. Check your solution.

$$c + 34 - 34 = 99 - 34 \qquad \text{Subtract 34 from each side of the equation.}$$
$$c = 65$$

Check: $c + 34 = 99$
$$65 + 34 \overset{?}{=} 99 \qquad \text{Replace } c \text{ with 65.}$$
$$99 = 99 \ ✔$$

Solve each equation. Check your solution.

1. $d + 22 = 60$

2. $s - 46 = 12$

3. $91 - t = 20$

4. $1.5 + r = 3$

5. $\$3.50 - g = \$1.25$

6. $x + 140 = 300$

7. $\$5.60 + h = \$7.00$

8. $e - 405 = 325$

9. $808 = p + 500$

10. $4.09 = 2 + y$

11. $11.3 = 15 - b$

12. $r - 2.2 = 6$

13. $a + 6.25 = 8.55$

14. $400 - m = 146$

15. $\$7.95 + n = \$10.00$

1-4 Practice

Solving Subtraction and Addition Equations

Solve each equation. Check your solution.

1. $62 - 35 = x$

2. $y + 16 = 47$

3. $z - 12 = 52$

4. $a - 12 = 13$

5. $16 = s + 9$

6. $12 = t - 4$

7. $22 = c - 12$

8. $34 = d + 16$

9. $20 + n = 40$

10. $p - 75 = 156$

11. $71 + 56 = s$

12. $15 + 72 = y$

13. $12 + n = 16$

14. $14 + q = 36$

15. $r - 18 = 36$

16. $f = 8.6 + 9.7$

17. $846 = n - 37$

18. $947 = p - 43$

19. $g - 6.3 = 9.5$

20. $h - 3.7 = 6.8$

21. $125 + y = 250$

22. $q = 387 + 221$

23. $7.36 + w = 8.94$

24. $2.17 + k = 4.19$

1-5 Study Guide

Solving Division and Multiplication Equations

You can use inverse operations to solve multiplication and division equations.

If you multiply each side of an equation by the same number, the two sides remain equal.

Example 1   Solve $y \div 6 = 7$. Check your solution.

$$y \div 6 \cdot 6 = 7 \cdot 6 \qquad \textit{Multiply each side of the equation by 6.}$$
$$y = 42$$

Check: $y \div 6 = 7$
$$42 \div 6 \overset{?}{=} 7 \qquad \textit{Replace y with 42.}$$
$$7 = 7 \; ✔$$

If you divide each side of an equation by the same number (not 0), the two sides remain equal.

Example 2   Solve $5m = 12.5$. Check your solution.

$$5m \div 5 = 12.5 \div 5 \qquad \textit{Divide each side of the equation by 5.}$$
$$m = 2.5$$

Check: $5m = 12.5$
$$5 \cdot 2.5 \overset{?}{=} 12.5 \qquad \textit{Replace m with 2.5.}$$
$$12.5 = 12.5 \; ✔$$

Solve each equation. Check your solution.

1. $14k = 84$

2. $\frac{b}{6} = 12$

3. $99 = 3e$

4. $15 = \frac{d}{7}$

5. $\$5.00 = 4w$

6. $9t = 729$

7. $3 = \frac{z}{22}$

8. $0.5p = 3$

9. $2.7 = 0.9r$

10. The product of 7 and a number w is 91. Find the number.

1-5 Practice

Solving Division and Multiplication Equations

Solve each equation. Check your solution.

1. $12x = 36$

2. $8y = 96$

3. $48 = 6y$

4. $54 = 9w$

5. $a \div 3 = 15$

6. $b \div 7 = 21$

7. $16y = 144$

8. $14b = 168$

9. $19z = 171$

10. $\frac{a}{12} = 16$

11. $\frac{c}{9} = 21$

12. $\frac{s}{6} = 12$

13. $21d = 147$

14. $125 \div 5 = a$

15. $63f = 945$

16. $\frac{h}{0.3} = 19$

17. $\frac{k}{2.7} = 21$

18. $\frac{m}{18} = 39$

19. $8.34x = 25.02$

20. $1.2y = 2.76$

21. $3.4t = 8.5$

22. $y = 17 \cdot 3$

23. $2.6v = 9.62$

24. $18t = 3.6$

25. $\frac{x}{1.8} = 72$

26. $\frac{n}{5} = 16.4$

27. $5.25a = 21$

28. $\frac{s}{1.5} = 24$

29. $6p = 17.94$

30. $\frac{10}{1.6} = m$

1-6 Study Guide

Writing Expressions and Equations

The table shows phrases written as mathematical expressions.

Phrase	Expression	Phrase	Expression
8 more than a number the sum of 8 and a number x plus 8 x increased by 8	$x + 8$	7 subtracted from a number h minus 7 7 less than a number a number decreased by 7	$h - 7$
Phrase	**Expression**	**Phrase**	**Expression**
3 multiplied by n 3 times a number the product of n and 3	$3n$	a number divided by 5 the quotient of t divided by 5 divide a number by 5	$\frac{t}{5}$

Write each phrase as an algebraic expression.

1. 12 more than a number

2. the quotient of a number divided by 9

3. 4 times a number

4. 15 less than a number

5. 1 less than the product of 3 and m

6. the product of 4 times a number minus 8

Write each sentence as an algebraic equation.

7. A number minus 6 equals 12.

8. A number plus 14 equals 25.

9. 3 more than 5 times the number of dogs is 18 dogs.

10. 4 times the number of cows plus 2 times the number of ducks is 20.

11. 2 less than the quotient of 12 divided by a number is 2.

12. The product of 5 and y added to 3 is 33.

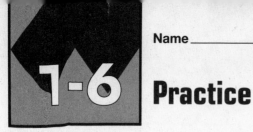

1-6 Practice

Writing Expressions and Equations

Write each phrase or sentence as an algebraic expression or equation.

1. 8 more than x

2. 12 less than b

3. the product of 6 and y

4. the quotient of a and 4

5. the sum of 9 and c

6. the difference of q and 12

7. 7 times d

8. 20 less n

9. 6 less than x is 18.

10. 4 more than y is 17.

11. The product of a and 7 is 21.

12. The sum of 1 and w is 12.

13. the sum of 8 and 6 times y

14. eight dollars less than Joni earned

15. Pak's salary minus a $223 deduction

16. twice as many flowers as Susan picked

17. 6 less than the product of 8 and c is 58.

18. The cost of the tea plus 10 cents tax is $2.09.

19. 8 more than the number of meals served on Tuesday

20. 18 less than the number of gameboard squares is 126.

21. 6 is 1 more than twice the number of miles Timothy drove.

22. The sum of 9 and the quotient of x and 7 is 11.

23. 12 less than twice the number of cows is 36.

24. 17 inches less than 3 times Maria's height is 169 inches.

25. 5 more than the number of paper clips divided into 4 groups

26. 8 more than 3 times Tony's wages

27. 1 less than the number of apples divided into 5 groups is 32.

1-7 Study Guide

Solving Two-Step Equations

To solve a two-step equation, undo each operation. First undo addition and subtraction. Then undo multiplication and division.

Examples   **1**   Solve $4k - 3 = 13$. Check your solution.

$$4k - 3 + 3 = 13 + 3$$ *Add 3 to each side to undo subtraction of 3.*
$$4k = 16$$
$$\frac{4k}{4} = \frac{16}{4}$$ *Divide each side by 4 to undo multiplication of 4.*
$$k = 4$$

Check: $4k - 3 = 13$
$4 \cdot 4 - 3 \stackrel{?}{=} 13$ *Replace k with 4.*
$16 - 3 \stackrel{?}{=} 13$ *Multiply first. Then subtract.*
$13 = 13$ ✔

2   Solve $\frac{r}{5} + 2 = 6$. Check your solution.

$$\frac{r}{5} + 2 - 2 = 6 - 2$$ *Subtract 2 from each side to undo addition of 2.*
$$\frac{r}{5} = 4$$
$$\frac{r}{5} \times 5 = 4 \times 5$$ *Multiply each side by 5 to undo division by 5.*
$$r = 20$$

Check: $\frac{r}{5} + 2 = 6$
$\frac{20}{5} + 2 \stackrel{?}{=} 6$ *Replace r with 20.*
$4 + 2 \stackrel{?}{=} 6$ *Divide first. Then add.*
$6 = 6$ ✔

Solve each equation. Check your solution.

1. $6t - 3 = 21$

2. $2m + 7 = 15$

3. $8 - 1.2y = 2$

4. $\frac{h}{3} - 5 = 2$

5. $\frac{v}{2} + 11 = 16$

6. $\frac{x}{7} + 1 = 4$

7. $9w - 7 = 74$

8. $50 - 3b = 35$

9. $\frac{n}{10} - 2.5 = 7.5$

10. $\frac{a}{7} - 13 = 12$

11. $6x - 12 = 78$

12. $7p + 8.4 = 8.4$

Mathematics: Applications and Connections, Course 3

1-7 Practice

Solving Two-Step Equations

Solve each equation. Check your solution.

1. $8x + 3 = 35$

2. $2y - 9 = 9$

3. $6a + 12 = 42$

4. $\frac{b}{4} - 2 = 8$

5. $\frac{w}{2} + 5 = 10$

6. $\frac{c}{7} - 3 = 0$

7. $8 + 5d = 53$

8. $12f - 9 = 27$

9. $7 + 8g = 87$

10. $6h + 3.7 = 51.7$

11. $7z - 9.4 = 11.6$

12. $4g + 0.7 = 36.7$

13. $2y - 3 = 9$

14. $6c + 4 = 58$

15. $9d - 8 = 154$

16. $9 + \frac{r}{5} = 15$

17. $\frac{s}{3} - 7 = 7$

18. $\frac{t}{6} + 12 = 24$

19. $74 = 14 + 5k$

20. $79 = 6t + 7$

21. $51 = 4m - 13$

22. $10 = 6 + \frac{t}{8}$

23. $4 = \frac{s}{5} - 16$

24. $\frac{u}{8} + 15 = 27$

25. $6x + 1.2 = 4.2$

26. $8y - 4.6 = 68.2$

27. $10f - 0.5 = 22.5$

28. $0.4m - 2.7 = 11.7$

29. $1.2n + 3.6 = 14.4$

30. $0.93 = 0.15 + 0.3w$

Mathematics: Applications and Connections, Course 3

1-8 Study Guide

Integration: Geometry
Perimeter and Area

Perimeter is the distance around the figure.
Area is the measure of the inside of the figure in square units.

Figure	Rectangle	Square	Parallelogram
Perimeter	$P = 2\ell + 2w$	$P = 4s$	$P = 2a + 2b$
Area	$A = \ell w$	$A = s^2$	$A = bh$
Example	$\ell = 9$ m $w = 4$ m $P = 2(9) + 2(4)$ $P = 18 + 8 = 26$ m $A = 9 \cdot 4$ $A = 36$ sq. m	$s = 8$ cm $P = 4 \times 8$ $P = 32$ cm $A = 8^2$ $A = 64$ sq. cm	$a = 7$ ft $h = 6$ ft $b = 5$ ft $P = 2(7) + 2(5)$ $P = 14 + 10 = 24$ ft $A = 5 \cdot 6$ $A = 30$ sq. ft

Find the perimeter and area of each figure.

1. 8 m
    5 m

2.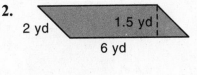
    2 yd   1.5 yd
    6 yd

3. 5.5 cm

4. 5 ft   3 ft
    9 ft
    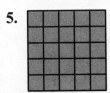

5.

6. 2.1 cm
    6.9 cm
    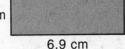

7. A rectangle is 18 feet long. Find its perimeter if its width is $\frac{1}{2}$ of its length.

8. Use an equation to find the width of a rectangle that has a length of 12 meters and an area of 84 square meters.

Mathematics: Applications and Connections, Course 3

1-8 Practice

Integration: Geometry
Perimeter and Area

Find the perimeter and area of each figure.

1.

2.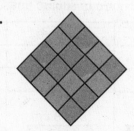

3.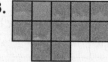

4.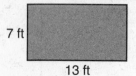
7 ft
13 ft

5.
12.5 yds
6 yd   9 yd

6.
25 cm
25 cm

7.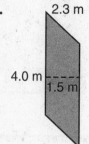
2.3 m
4.0 m
1.5 m

8.
6.4 in.
6.4 in.

9.
50 ft
25 ft

10.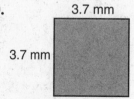
3.7 mm
3.7 mm

11.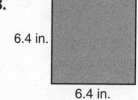
10.5 in.
17.5 in.
35 in.

12.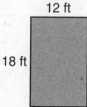
12 ft
18 ft

Mathematics: Applications and Connections, Course 3

1-9 Study Guide

Solving Inequalities

The symbol $>$ means **greater than.** The symbol $<$ means **less than.**
Inequalities are sentences that contains $>$ or $<$.

Symbols	Words
$2r + 1 > 5$	$2r + 1$ is greater than 5.
$w - 6 < 9$	$w - 6$ is less than 9.

An inequality has more than one solution.

Example   **Solve $2r + 1 > 5$. Show the solution on a number line.**

$2r + 1 - 1 > 5 - 1$ *Undo addition.*
$2r > 4$

$\frac{2r}{2} > \frac{4}{2}$ *Undo multiplication.*

$r > 2$

To graph the solution on a number line, draw a circle at 2. Then draw an
arrow to show all numbers greater than 2.

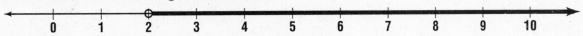

Solve each inequality. Graph the solution on a number line.

1. $y + 7 < 12$

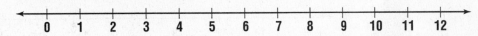

2. $2t - 1 > 9$

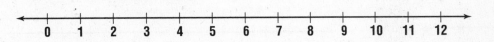

3. $m - 3 < 8$

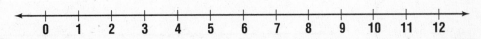

4. $6w > 18$

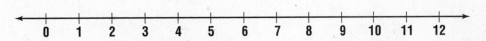

5. $1 + 2h < 15$

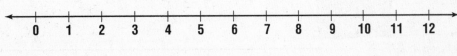

6. $\frac{e}{2} > 3$

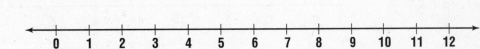

*Mathematics: Applications
and Connections,* Course 3

1-9 **Practice**

Solving Inequalities

Solve each inequality. Show the solution on the number line.

1. $x + 2 > 6$

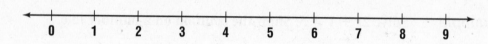

2. $y + 3 < 9$

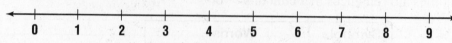

3. $3 \cdot e > 12$

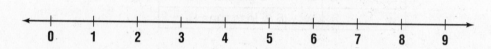

4. $\frac{f}{4} > 2$

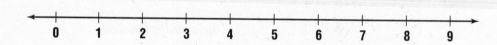

5. $a + 12 < 18$

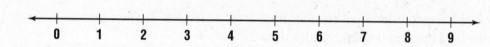

6. $b - 2 < 6$

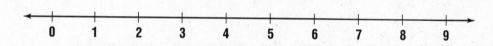

7. $4c < 8$

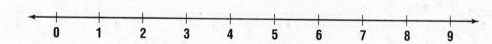

8. $\frac{d}{3} > 3$

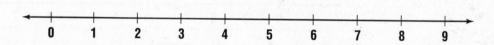

9. $2x + 3 > 9$

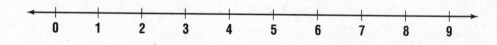

10. $4y - 6 < 18$

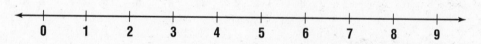

11. $\frac{t}{2} + 6 < 8$

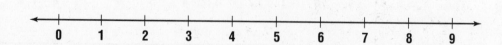

2-1 Study Guide

Integers and Absolute Value

Positive and negative whole numbers are called **integers**.

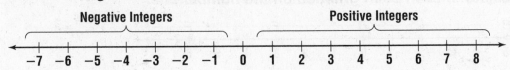

The **absolute value** of a number is the distance the number is from zero on the number line.

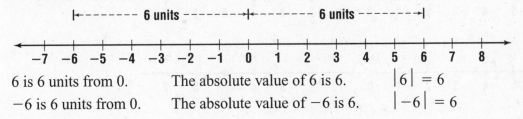

6 is 6 units from 0.   The absolute value of 6 is 6. $|6| = 6$

−6 is 6 units from 0.   The absolute value of −6 is 6. $|-6| = 6$

Graph each set of points on the number line.

1. $\{-6, -3, 2, 5\}$

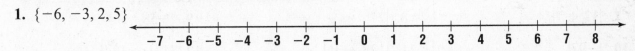

2. $\{-2, -4, 0, -6\}$

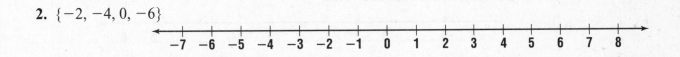

3. $\{5, 7, -3, -4\}$

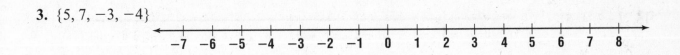

4. $\{0, -1, 1, -5\}$

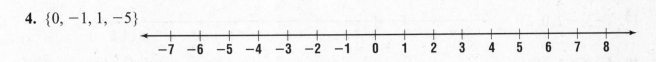

Find each absolute value.

5. $|19|$

6. $|-21|$

7. $|-8|$

8. $|15 + 15|$

Mathematics: Applications and Connections, Course 3

2-1 Practice

Integers and Absolute Value

Name the coordinate of each point graphed on the number line.

1.
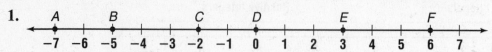

2.
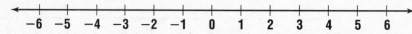

3.
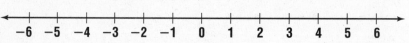

Find each absolute value.

4. $|0|$

5. $|-13|$

6. $|6|$

7. $|12 + 7|$

8. $|27|$

9. $|-58|$

10. $|-97|$

11. $|128 - 36|$

12. $|421 + 124|$

Graph each set of points on the number line.

13. $\{-3, -1, 0\}$
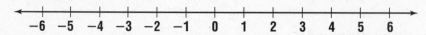

14. $\{2, 5, 6\}$

15. $\{-3, 4, 5\}$

16. $\{-4, -5, -6\}$

17. $\{-3, -2, 0, 2\}$

18. $\{-5, -2, 2, 5\}$

19. $\{-2, -1, 0, 2\}$

20. $\{-4, -1, 0, 1\}$

Mathematics: Applications and Connections, Course 3

2-2 **Study Guide**

Comparing and Ordering Integers

To compare integers, think of a number line. The number farther to the
right on the number line is greater.

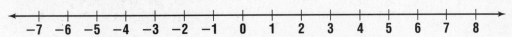

Examples *Use the number line to compare integers.*
Replace each ◯ *with >, <, or =.*

1 −7 ◯ 7   *A negative integer is less than a positive integer.*
−7 < 7

2 −4 ◯ −6   *−4 is to the right of −6 on the number line.*
−4 > −6

3 2 ◯ |−2| *The absolute value of −2 is 2.*
2 = |−2|

Replace each ◯ **with >, <, or = to make a true sentence.**

1. −9 ◯ 7   **2.** 0 ◯ −5   **3.** −43 ◯ −34

4. |4| ◯ −4   **5.** |−7| ◯ |7| **6.** 12 ◯ −12

7. |−1| ◯ 0   **8.** |−20| ◯ |20| **9.** −72 ◯ −50

Order the integers in each set from least to greatest.

10. {17, 12, 1, −9, −6}

11. {−67, 0, −45, −53, −43, 45}

Order the integers in each set from greatest to least.

12. {90, −180, −60, 65, 0, −11}

13. {−74, 47, −89, 13, 31, −8}

2-2 Practice

Comparing and Ordering Integers

Replace each ◯ with >, <, or = to make a true sentence.

1. 46 ◯ 53   **2.** −19 ◯ 18   **3.** 47 ◯ −28

4. 0 ◯ 13   **5.** −8 ◯ 0   **6.** 0 ◯ −27

7. −6 ◯ −5   **8.** −7 ◯ 7   **9.** 9 ◯ −4

10. −46 ◯ 46   **11.** 45 ◯ 45   **12.** 45 ◯ −45

13. 90 ◯ −101   **14.** −10 ◯ 10   **15.** |−12| ◯ 12

16. |36| ◯ |−36| **17.** |−34| ◯ |−6| **18.** |0| ◯ 0

19. |15| ◯ |13| **20.** |−12| ◯ |12| **21.** |−622| ◯ 0

Order the integers in each set from least to greatest.

22. {−3, 4, −5, 6}

23. {−4, 4, −5, 5, 9}

24. {−66, −98, 47, 0, 13, 28}

25. {0, 5, 8, −361, 224}

26. {−54, −56, 55, 9, 53, 51}

Order the integers in each set from greatest to least.

27. {−3, 7, 0, −2, 8}

28. {0, 99, 16, 87, 12, −14}

29. {261, −384, 275, −288}

30. {−61, −123, −75, −126}

*Mathematics: Applications
and Connections, Course 3*

2-3 Study Guide

Adding Integers

You can use a number line to add integers. Locate the first addend on the number line. Move right if the second addend is positive. Move left if the second addend is negative.

Example 1   Solve $d = 4 + (-10)$.

Start at 4. Since -10 is negative, move left 10 units.

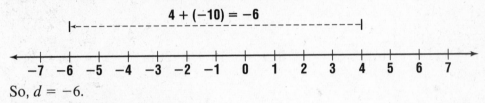

$$4 + (-10) = -6$$

So, $d = -6$.

When you add integers, remember the following.

The sum of two positive integers is positive.
The sum of two negative integers is negative.
The sum of a positive integer and a negative integer is positive if the positive integer has the greater absolute value and negative if the negative integer has the greater absolute value.

Examples   **2** Solve $t = 24 + (-13)$.

$|24| > |-13|$, so the sum is positive.
The difference of 24 and 13 is 11, so $t = 11$.

3 Solve $-17 + 16 = m$.

$|-17| > |16|$, so the sum is negative.
The difference of 17 and 16 is 1, so $m = -1$.

Solve each equation.

1. $h = 15 + (-10)$

2. $-20 + (-9) = g$

3. $s = -9 + 39$

4. $-50 + 20 = p$

5. $y = -11 + (-19)$

6. $z = 12 + 15$

7. $500 + (-250) = w$

8. $e = 48 + (-8)$

9. $-80 + (-20) = v$

10. $t = -109 + 49$

11. $544 + 206 = b$

12. $4 + (-16) = d$

Evaluate each expression if $a = 10$, $b = -10$, and $c = 5$.

13. $a + 23$

14. $b + (-7)$

15. $b + c$

16. $-20 + c$

17. $a + (-56)$

18. $23 + b$

2-3 Practice

Adding Integers

Solve each equation.

1. $16 + (-8) = a$

2. $q = -12 + (-12)$

3. $36 + 16 = m$

4. $-19 + 0 = p$

5. $-35 + 45 = v$

6. $n = 53 + (-63)$

7. $w = 111 + (-112)$

8. $r = -16 + (-20)$

9. $-14 + 50 = x$

10. $a = 16 + (-36)$

11. $28 + 42 = u$

12. $-31 + (-46) = b$

13. $v = 21 + (-18)$

14. $c = -8 + 34$

15. $-12 + (-16) = w$

16. $74 + (-63) = d$

17. $x = -95 + (-46)$

18. $e = 81 + 63$

19. $-57 + 86 = y$

20. $-14 + (-98) = f$

21. $z = 47 + (-63)$

22. $k = -125 + 79$

23. $-32 + (-89) = w$

Evaluate each expression if r = 3, t = −3, and w = −5.

24. $r + 12$

25. $w + (-8)$

26. $t + r$

Mathematics: Applications and Connections, Course 3

2-4 Study Guide

More About Adding Integers

You can use the associative property and the commutative property to help add integers.

Associative Property: Addends may be grouped in any way. The sum will remain the same.

Example 1 Solve $m = -4 + (-6) + 9$.

$$m = [-4 + (-6)] + 9$$
$$m = -10 + 9$$
$$m = -1$$

Check: $m = -4 + (-6) + 9$

$$m = -4 + [(-6) + 9]$$
$$m = -4 + 3$$
$$m = -1$$

Commutative Property: Integers may be added in any order. The sum will remain the same.

Example 2 Solve $y = 40 + (-25) + 60$.

$$y = 40 + 60 + (-25)$$
$$y = 100 + (-25)$$
$$y = 75$$

Check: *Use the associative property.*

$$y = [40 + (-25)] + 60$$
$$y = 15 + 60$$
$$y = 75$$

Solve each equation. Check by solving another way.

1. $h = 7 + (-8) + (-7)$

2. $-20 + 5 + (-10) + 3 = n$

3. $r = 6 + (-9) + 11$

4. $-9 + (-3) + 12 + (-3) = f$

5. $c = 10 + (-15) + (-8) + 7$

6. $-6 + (-6) + 6 = k$

7. $v = 26 + 24 + (-16) + (-1)$

8. $(-11) + 15 + (-4) + 3 = g$

9. $x = -7 + (-8) + 15$

Evaluate each expression if $m = -5$, $n = 7$, and $p = 10$.

10. $m + (-9) + p$

11. $-10 + n + p + (-7)$

12. $(-8) + m + (-1)$

2-4 Practice

More About Adding Integers

Solve each equation.

1. $a = 3 + (-7) + 12$

2. $(-6) + 17 + 3 = d$

3. $x = (-8) + 5 + 19$

4. $z = (-3) + (-8) + (-9)$

Solve each equation. Check by solving another way.

5. $w = 35 + (-8) + 54$

6. $51 + (-7) + (-17) = k$

7. $27 + (-35) + 23 + (-15) = g$

8. $m = (-32) + 16 + 18 + 43$

9. $e = 41 + 26 + (-35) + 18$

10. $n = -14 + (-18) + 19 + 16$

11. $t = -63 + 18 + (-37) + 21$

12. $42 + (-43) + 45 + (-46) = d$

13. $75 + (-100) + 75 + (-50) = y$

14. $m = -38 + 12 + (-10) + 15$

15. $w = -9 + (-7) + (-10) + (-6)$

16. $45 + 52 + (-32) + 55 = p$

Evaluate each expression if c = 4, x = −5, and h = 6.

17. $x + 5 + 9 + (-7)$

18. $(-12) + c + (-3)$

19. $h + c + x + (-12) + 8$

20. $-6 + x + h$

21. $-12 + h + x + h$

22. $(c + c) + x$

2-5 Study Guide

Subtracting Integers

An integer and its **opposite** are the same distance from 0 on a number line.
4 and -4 are opposites.

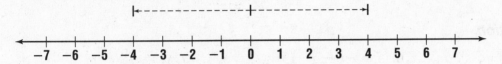

The sum of an integer and its opposite is 0. $-4 + 4 = 0$

To subtract an integer, add its opposite.

Examples

1 Solve $4 - 8 = y$.

$$4 - 8 = y \qquad \textit{To subtract 8,}$$
$$4 + (-8) = y \qquad \textit{add } -8.$$
$$-4 = y$$

2 Solve $4 - (-4) = x$.

$$4 - (-4) = x \qquad \textit{To subtract } -4,$$
$$4 + 4 = x \qquad \textit{add 4.}$$
$$8 = x$$

Solve each equation.

1. $b = 16 - (-3)$

2. $n = -8 - 25$

3. $w = -11 - (-6)$

4. $-19 - (-3) = h$

5. $65 - (-45) = k$

6. $-19 - 20 = c$

7. $s = 100 - (-72)$

8. $z = -44 - (-33)$

9. $d = 89 - 17$

10. $-80 - (-35) = p$

11. $98 - (-90) = f$

12. $-75 - 23 = g$

Evaluate each expression if $w = -9$, $x = 3$, and $y = -8$.

13. $60 - w$

14. $12 - y$

15. $x - (-12)$

16. $w - x$

17. $y - w$

18. $x - y$

19. $-31 - y$

20. $w - 50$

21. $12 - x$

2-5 Practice

Subtracting Integers

Write the additive inverse of each integer.

1. -18 **2.** 12 **3.** -36 **4.** 61

Solve each equation.

5. $a = 5 - (-3)$ **6.** $e = -6 - (-13)$ **7.** $d = -8 - 17$

8. $-2 - 16 = g$ **9.** $b = 15 - (-15)$ **10.** $42 - (-91) = k$

11. $a = 30 - (-12)$ **12.** $e = (-27) - (-18)$ **13.** $-51 - (-18) = h$

14. $63 - (-27) = f$ **15.** $81 - 98 = g$ **16.** $m = -16 - (-16)$

17. $b = -41 - (-86)$ **18.** $h = 273 - 421$ **19.** $n = (-361) - 684$

20. $c = -847 - 98$ **21.** $j = 647 - (-77)$ **22.** $427 - 847 = p$

Evaluate each expression if $y = -6$, $p = 8$, and $x = -10$.

23. $86 - x$ **24.** $y - (-19)$ **25.** $46 - p$

26. $y + p - x$ **27.** $p + x - y$ **28.** $100 - (y + p + x)$

2-6 Study Guide

Integration: Statistics
Matrices

A **matrix** is a rectangular arrangement of numbers in *rows* and *columns*.
Each number in a matrix is called an **element** of the matrix.

You can add or subtract matrices that have the same number of rows and
columns. Add and subtract matrices by adding or subtracting the
corresponding elements.

Examples Find each sum or difference.

1 $\begin{bmatrix} 8 & -2 \\ 7 & 3 \end{bmatrix} + \begin{bmatrix} 4 & 1 \\ 6 & 5 \end{bmatrix}$

$\begin{bmatrix} 8 & -2 \\ 7 & 3 \end{bmatrix} + \begin{bmatrix} 4 & 1 \\ 6 & 5 \end{bmatrix} = \begin{bmatrix} 8+4 & -2+1 \\ 7+6 & 3+5 \end{bmatrix} = \begin{bmatrix} 12 & -1 \\ 13 & 8 \end{bmatrix}$

2 $\begin{bmatrix} 15 & 0 \\ 12 & -9 \end{bmatrix} - \begin{bmatrix} -3 & 2 \\ 6 & -4 \end{bmatrix}$

$\begin{bmatrix} 15 & 0 \\ 12 & -9 \end{bmatrix} - \begin{bmatrix} -3 & 2 \\ 6 & -4 \end{bmatrix} = \begin{bmatrix} 15-(-3) & 0-2 \\ 12-6 & -9-(-4) \end{bmatrix} = \begin{bmatrix} 18 & -2 \\ 6 & -5 \end{bmatrix}$

Find each sum or difference.

1. $\begin{bmatrix} 10 & -3 \\ 5 & 8 \end{bmatrix} + \begin{bmatrix} -2 & -12 \\ 20 & 22 \end{bmatrix}$

2. $\begin{bmatrix} 3 & -2 \\ 1 & 2 \end{bmatrix} - \begin{bmatrix} 1 & 1 \\ -5 & -6 \end{bmatrix}$

3. $\begin{bmatrix} 8 & -2 \\ 7 & 3 \end{bmatrix} + \begin{bmatrix} 4 & 1 \\ 6 & 5 \end{bmatrix}$

4. $\begin{bmatrix} 15 & 0 \\ 12 & -9 \end{bmatrix} - \begin{bmatrix} -3 & 2 \\ 6 & -4 \end{bmatrix}$

5. $\begin{bmatrix} 5 & -4 & 35 \\ 2 & -2 & 16 \end{bmatrix} - \begin{bmatrix} 1 & 4 & -35 \\ -2 & 2 & 0 \end{bmatrix}$

6. $\begin{bmatrix} 2 & -1 \\ 3 & 7 \\ 14 & -9 \end{bmatrix} + \begin{bmatrix} -6 & 9 \\ 7 & -11 \\ -8 & 17 \end{bmatrix}$

2-6 Practice

Integration: Statistics
Matrices

Find each sum or difference. If there is no sum or difference, write impossible.

1. $\begin{bmatrix} 3 & -2 \\ 4 & 8 \end{bmatrix} + \begin{bmatrix} -1 & 7 \\ 3 & 8 \end{bmatrix}$

2. $\begin{bmatrix} 0 & 8 & 4 \\ -5 & -6 & -1 \end{bmatrix} + \begin{bmatrix} -3 & 6 & 1 \\ 2 & -5 & 9 \end{bmatrix}$

3. $[7 \ -4 \ 8] - [-1 \ 2 \ 4]$

4. $[3 \ -2 \ -7] - \begin{bmatrix} 9 \\ -2 \\ -6 \end{bmatrix}$

5. $\begin{bmatrix} 4 & 12 & -4 \\ 0 & 5 & -6 \\ -1 & -4 & -3 \end{bmatrix} + \begin{bmatrix} 9 & -1 \\ -3 & -8 \\ 7 & 17 \end{bmatrix}$

6. $\begin{bmatrix} 12 & 7 & 4 \\ 23 & 9 & 1 \\ 0 & 3 & 8 \end{bmatrix} - \begin{bmatrix} 5 & 15 & 8 \\ 6 & 3 & 4 \\ -2 & -3 & -7 \end{bmatrix}$

7. $\begin{bmatrix} 2 \\ -6 \end{bmatrix} - \begin{bmatrix} 5 \\ -7 \end{bmatrix}$

8. $\begin{bmatrix} 15 & 7 \\ 30 & -12 \end{bmatrix} - \begin{bmatrix} -5 & 29 \\ -6 & 10 \end{bmatrix}$

9. $\begin{bmatrix} 27 & -23 & 15 \\ 8 & 3 & -3 \\ 6 & -12 & 13 \end{bmatrix} + \begin{bmatrix} 5 & 9 & -31 \\ 8 & 4 & 12 \\ -4 & -7 & 8 \end{bmatrix}$

10. $\begin{bmatrix} 4 & -6 \\ 5 & 9 \\ -2 & 1 \end{bmatrix} + \begin{bmatrix} 5 & 1 & 2 \\ -2 & 7 & -3 \\ 5 & 7 & 8 \end{bmatrix}$

2-7 Study Guide

Multiplying Integers

The product of two positive integers is positive.

Examples
$k = 4(9)$
$k = 36$

$m = 6(7)(2)$
$m = 42(2)$
$m = 84$

$j = 5(3)(5)$
$j = 15(5)$
$j = 75$

The product of two negative integers is positive.

Examples
$h = (-7)(-5)$
$h = 35$

$v = (-9)^2$
$v = -9(-9)$
$v = 81$

$z = (-25)(-7)$
$z = 175$

The product of a positive integer and a negative integer is negative.

Examples
$c = (-20)(8)$
$c = -160$

$g = (70)(-3)(2)$
$g = -210(2)$
$g = -420$

$y = (-6)(5)^2$
$y = (-6)25$
$y = -150$

Solve each equation.

1. $z = 8(9)$

2. $t = -4(8)$

3. $b = 4(-5)$

4. $-5(-5) = h$

5. $-40(6) = n$

6. $20(-9) = y$

7. $2(-5)(-8) = h$

8. $g = -6(-3)(-2)$

9. $w = -5(10)(-4)$

10. $t = (-20)^2$

11. $-10(9)^2 = p$

12. $r = (5)^2 \cdot (-10)^2$

Evaluate each expression if $q = -4$, $r = -8$, and $s = 10$.

13. $2qr$

14. $-10sq$

15. $-8s^2$

16. qrs

17. $-3sr$

18. $5r^2$

2-7 Practice

Multiplying Integers

Solve each equation.

1. $(-3)(-6) = x$

2. $5(-4) = m$

3. $p = 6(8)$

4. $a = 9(-5)$

5. $h = 7(-15)$

6. $n = (-7)(-12)$

7. $e = (-16)(-4)$

8. $(-12)(3) = j$

9. $r = -14(-8)$

10. $g = 14(36)$

11. $k = -11(-11)$

12. $s = -16(-21)$

13. $b = -16(9)$

14. $-14(-12) = k$

15. $t = -18(0)$

16. $-21(-8) = d$

17. $q = -26(7)$

18. $u = -33(-9)$

19. $r = (-2)(8)(-4)$

20. $s = (4)(0)(9)$

21. $(-3)(-4)(-5) = z$

22. $c = (-2)(8)(-90)$

23. $m = (-18)^2$

24. $8(3)(16) = w$

25. $f = (-2)(8)(-5)^2$

26. $p = (4)(-11)(3)$

27. $x = (4)^2 \cdot (-2)^2$

Evaluate each expression if $a = -2$, $b = -5$, and $c = 8$.

28. $6ab$

29. $-4bc$

30. bc^2

Mathematics: Applications and Connections, Course 3

2-8 Study Guide

Dividing Integers

If two integers have the same sign, their quotient is positive.

Examples $m = 420 \div 7$ *The signs are the same.*
$m = 60$ *The quotient is positive.*

$d = 290 \div 29$ *The signs are the same.*
$d = 10$ *The quotient is positive.*

If two integers have different signs, their quotient is negative.

Examples $f = -25 \div 5$ *The signs are different.*
$f = -5$ *The quotient is negative.*

$a = \frac{20}{-4}$ *The signs are different.*

$a = -5$ *The quotient is negative.*

Solve each equation.

1. $81 \div -9 = c$

2. $r = \frac{-72}{8}$

3. $b = 680 \div 4$

4. $-325 \div (-5) = p$

5. $-700 \div 35 = y$

6. $t = -560 \div (-80)$

7. $k = \frac{285}{19}$

8. $-96 \div (-32) = g$

9. $840 \div (-7) = z$

10. $-189 \div 9 = j$

11. $m = 248 \div (-4)$

12. $z = 408 \div 51$

Evaluate each expression if $q = -48$, $r = 6$, and $t = -12$.

13. $-108 \div t$

14. $\frac{q}{-8}$

15. $312 \div r$

16. $\frac{q}{r}$

17. $6r \div t$

18. $-144 \div t$

2-8 Practice

Dividing Integers

Solve each equation.

1. $\frac{-27}{9} = b$

2. $v = \frac{42}{-7}$

3. $n = \frac{-63}{-9}$

4. $t = -42 \div 14$

5. $-12 \div (-4) = z$

6. $16 \div (-8) = p$

7. $m = 120 \div (-20)$

8. $n = -240 \div (-4)$

9. $p = -64 \div (-8)$

10. $a = \frac{-366}{3}$

11. $b = \frac{-144}{-6}$

12. $c = \frac{-80}{16}$

13. $\frac{-121}{-11} = w$

14. $\frac{-240}{8} = x$

15. $\frac{440}{-20} = y$

16. $315 \div 9 = p$

17. $-312 \div (-12) = q$

18. $285 \div (-15) = r$

19. $d = -312 \div (-6)$

20. $e = 232 \div (-8)$

21. $f = -144 \div (-9)$

22. $h = \frac{516}{12}$

23. $j = \frac{-430}{10}$

24. $g = \frac{-344}{-8}$

25. $q = \frac{-630}{42}$

26. $-360 \div 8 = r$

27. $\frac{-4,096}{-64} = s$

Evaluate each expression if c = −3, r = 9, and t = −10.

28. $\frac{200}{t}$

29. $\frac{162}{r}$

30. $\frac{63}{c}$

31. $cr \div 3$

32. $tr \div c$

33. $(crt)^2 \div 6$

Mathematics: Applications and Connections, Course 3

2-9 Study Guide

Solving Equations

Integer equations are solved like whole-number equations. For addition or subtraction equations, add or subtract the same number on both sides of the equation. Watch for signs. Use the additive inverse to simplify equations.

Examples   **1**   Solve $k + 16 = -20$.

$$k + 16 = -20$$
$$k + 16 - 16 = -20 - 16$$
$$k = -36$$

2   Solve $c - (-21) = 40$.

$$c - (-21) = 40$$
$$c + 21 = 40$$
$$c + 21 - 21 = 40 - 21$$
$$c = 19$$

For multiplication and division equations, multiply or divide both sides of the equation by the same number.

Examples   **3**   Solve $-7t = -98$.

$$-7t = -98$$
$$-7t \div (-7) = -98 \div (-7)$$
$$t = 14$$

4   Solve $\frac{m}{20} = -4$.

$$\frac{m}{20} = -4$$
$$\frac{m}{20} \cdot 20 = -4\,(20)$$
$$m = -80$$

For two-step equations, work backwards. Add or subtract first. Then multiply or divide.

Examples   **5**   Solve $3x - 7 = -19$.

$$3x - 7 = -19$$
$$3x - 7 + 7 = -19 + 7$$
$$3x = -12$$
$$x = -4$$

6   Solve $\frac{v}{3} - (-2) = 7$.

$$\frac{v}{3} - (-2) = 7$$
$$\frac{v}{3} + 2 = 7$$
$$\frac{v}{3} + 2 - 2 = 7 - 2$$
$$\frac{v}{3} = 5$$
$$\frac{v}{3} \cdot 3 = 5(3)$$
$$v = 15$$

Solve each equation. Check your solution.

1. $7z = -49$

2. $m \div 9 = -50$

3. $y - (-22) = 50$

4. $17 = k - (-8)$

5. $-60 = -3f$

6. $-70 = \frac{b}{5}$

7. $p - 10 = -33$

8. $-145 = w + 1$

9. $2h + (-2) = 18$

10. $\frac{n}{5} + 5 = 3$

11. $2y - 1 = -7$

12. $-99 = -33 + g$

2-9 Practice

Solving Equations

Solve each equation. Check your solution.

1. $x - 16 = -38$

2. $2w = -64$

3. $-9s = -63$

4. $y - (-12) = 16$

5. $-15 + a = -32$

6. $q + (-63) = -100$

7. $\frac{k}{5} = 18$

8. $\frac{m}{-6} = -9$

9. $x - 240 = 78$

10. $-17 = \frac{n}{4} - 13$

11. $25 = \frac{n}{-6} + (-19)$

12. $-6y = -960$

13. $18w = -234$

14. $2{,}294 = -74t$

15. $49 = -9y - 68$

16. $375 = 14x + (-17)$

17. $-12y - 14 = 142$

18. $15x + 36 = -249$

19. $9x + 63 = 135$

20. $12x - 9 = -141$

21. $4c + (-6) = 250$

22. $\frac{a}{-12} + 5 = 10$

23. $5s + 30 = -75$

24. $\frac{w}{7} + 9 = -3$

25. $10t - 45 = -105$

26. $16 + \frac{n}{-8} = -6$

27. $-6c - 5 = -215$

Mathematics: Applications
and Connections, Course 3

Study Guide

Name _____ **Date** _____

2-10

Integration: Geometry
Coordinate System

You can graph a point in the coordinate plane
using an ordered pair of numbers.

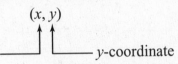

x-coordinate ——————————— y-coordinate

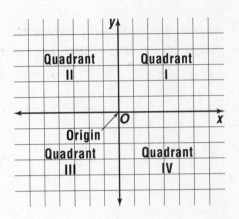

Examples

1 **Graph the point at $(-3, 2)$ on the grid below.**

Start at the origin. The
x-coordinate is -3. Move 3 units
to the left on the x-axis, the
horizontal axis.

The y-coordinate is 2. Move 2 units
up along the y-axis, the vertical
axis. Draw a point to show $(-3, 2)$.

2 **Name the ordered pair for point A.**

Find the point on the x-axis that
intersects the vertical line through
point A. The x-coordinate is 4.

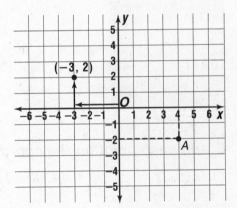

Find the point on the y-axis that
intersects the horizontal line
through point A. The y-coordinate
is -2. The ordered pair for point A
is $(4, -2)$.

**Name the ordered pair for the coordinates of
each point graphed on the coordinate plane.**

1. J 2. F 3. H

4. C 5. A 6. E

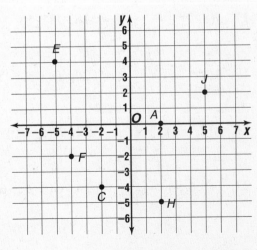

Graph each point on the same coordinate plane.

7. $B(0, 5)$ 8. $G(3, 4)$ 9. $K(2, -2)$

10. $L(-5, -5)$ 11. $I(-2, 1)$ 12. $D(6, -2)$

© Glencoe/McGraw-Hill

19

*Mathematics: Applications
and Connections,* Course 3

2-10 Practice

Integration: Geometry
The Coordinate System

Name the ordered pair for the coordinates of each point graphed on the coordinate plane.

1. A 2. J 3. F

4. H 5. B 6. G

7. E 8. K 9. C

10. M 11. D 12. N

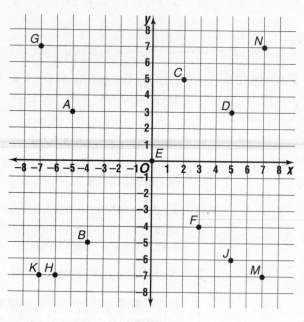

Graph each point on the coordinate plane.

13. $E(5, 2)$ 14. $K(-3, -1)$

15. $C(-4, 6)$ 16. $A(0, 0)$

17. $J(8, 7)$ 18. $F(7, 8)$

19. $M(4, -6)$ 20. $D(-5, -5)$

21. $N(2, -5)$ 22. $H(5, -6)$

23. $B(-6, 4)$ 24. $G(-2, -6)$

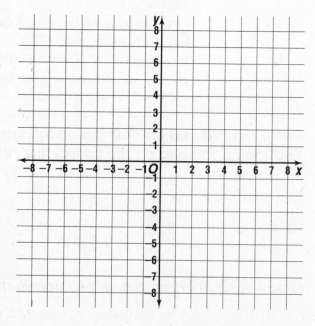

Mathematics: Applications and Connections, Course 3

3-1 Study Guide

Ratios and Rates

A **ratio** is a comparison of two numbers by division.

Examples   **Express each ratio in simplest form.**

1 35 wins to 42 losses   *The greatest common factor of 35 and 42 is 7.*

$\frac{35}{42} = \frac{5}{6}$ *Divide the numerator and denominator by 7.*

The ratio in simplest form is $\frac{5}{6}$ or 5 : 6.

2 1 foot to 3 inches

$\frac{1 \text{ foot}}{3 \text{ inches}} = \frac{12 \text{ inches}}{3 \text{ inches}}$ *The greatest common factor of 12 and 3 is 3.*

$\frac{4 \text{ inches}}{1 \text{ inch}}$ *Divide the numerator and denominator by 3.*

The ratio in simplest form is $\frac{4}{1}$ or 4 to 1.

A **rate** is a ratio that compares two different units.

Example 3   **Express** *Andres drove 300 miles in 6 hours* **as a unit rate.**

$\frac{300 \text{ miles}}{6 \text{ hours}} = \frac{50 \text{ miles}}{1 \text{ hour}}$ *Divide the numerator and denominator by 6.*

Andres drove at a rate of 50 miles per hour.

Express each ratio or rate in simplest form.

1. 12 wins:15 games

2. 8 out of 20 cars

3. 65 to 10

4. 8 out of 10 people

5. 90 men:144 women

6. 81 to 36

7. 180 tickets:60 tickets

8. 4 feet:1 yard

9. 3 out of 24

Express each rate as a unit rate.

10. $45 for 9 hours

11. 280 kilometers in 5 hours

12. $330 for 3 days

13. 432 beats in 6 minutes

14. 77 pounds in 11 weeks

15. 480 miles in 12 hours

Mathematics: Applications and Connections, Course 3

Name _____ **Date** _____

3-1 Practice

Ratios and Rates

Express each ratio or rate in simplest form.

1. 9 to 28

2. 30 out of 50 doctors

3. 84 students to 3 teachers

4. 22 players:2 teams

5. 15:50

6. 19 out of 76

7. 20 wins in 32 games

8. 4 boys to 6 girls

9. 5 days per calendar year

10. $8 for 2 tickets

11. 14 wins:35 losses

12. 40 minutes per hour

13. 12 students:$54

14. 18 inches:1 yard

15. 6 hits to 14 times at bat

16. 1 inch per 1 foot

Express each rate as a unit rate.

17. 104 miles in 8 hours

18. 124 cubic yards to 62 carts

19. $84 saved in 7 weeks

20. 108 students in 3 classrooms

21. $10.81 for 23 pounds

22. $269.95 for 9 tickets

23. $11.97 for 9 gallons

24. $12.25 for 35 newspapers

© Glencoe/McGraw-Hill

20

Mathematics: Applications and Connections, Course 3

3-2 Study Guide

Ratios and Percents

A **percent** is a ratio that compares a number to 100.

Examples   **Express each ratio as a percent.**

> **1** He made **65 out of 100 foul shots.**
>
> 65 out of 100 = 65%
>
> **2** In 1992, $\frac{1}{4}$ of all high school students took physics.

$$\frac{1}{4} = \frac{25}{100} \qquad \text{So, } \frac{1}{4} = 25\%.$$

with $\times 25$ shown on numerator and denominator.

You can express a percent as a fraction by writing it as a fraction with a denominator of 100.

Example 3   **Express 95% as a fraction.**

$$95\% = \frac{95}{100}$$
$$= \frac{17}{20} \qquad \textit{Divide the numerator and the denominator by 5.}$$
$$\text{So, } 95\% = \frac{17}{20}.$$

Express each ratio or fraction as a percent.

1. $\frac{13}{65}$

2. 49 out of 98

3. 91 hundredths

4. 16 out of 25

5. $72\frac{1}{2}$ out of 100

6. $25 per $40

Express each percent as a fraction in simplest form.

7. 20%

8. 24%

9. 35%

10. 47%

11. 48%

12. 70%

Mathematics: Applications and Connections, Course 3

3-2 Practice

Ratios and Percents

Express each ratio or fraction as a percent.

1. 16 out of 25

2. 23:100

3. 2 in 50

4. 12 out of 30

5. $\frac{1}{4}$

6. 9 in 90

7. 87 out of 100

8. $\frac{1}{5}$

9. 6 in 12

10. 75 out of 150

Express each percent as a fraction in simplest form.

11. 85%

12. 26%

13. 3%

14. 10%

15. 75%

16. 65%

17. 81%

18. 15%

19. 38%

20. 68%

3-3 Study Guide

Solving Proportions

A **proportion** is an equation that shows that two ratios are equivalent. To determine if a pair of ratios form a proportion, find the *cross products*.

Examples   Determine whether each pair of ratios forms a proportion.

   1 $\frac{30}{48}$ and $\frac{15}{24}$

   Find the cross products.

   $30 \times 24 = 720$ $48 \times 15 = 720$

   Since the cross products are equal, the ratios form a proportion.

   2 $\frac{20}{24}$ and $\frac{12}{18}$

   Find the cross products.

   $20 \times 18 = 360$ $24 \times 12 = 288$

   Since the cross products are not equal, the ratios do not form a proportion.

You can also use cross products to solve proportions.

Example 3   Solve $\frac{12}{30}$ and $\frac{k}{70}$.

   $30 \times k = 12 \times 70$
   $30k = 840$
   $k = 28$ The solution is 28.

Determine whether each pair of ratios forms a proportion.

1. $\frac{4}{6}, \frac{16}{24}$ **2.** $\frac{15}{25}, \frac{10}{20}$ **3.** $\frac{9}{12}, \frac{10}{15}$ **4.** $\frac{27}{72}, \frac{12}{32}$

5. $\frac{7}{15}, \frac{13}{32}$ **6.** $\frac{10}{24}, \frac{6}{14}$ **7.** $\frac{32}{12}, \frac{56}{21}$ **8.** $\frac{15}{6}, \frac{10}{3}$

Solve each proportion.

9. $\frac{3}{4} = \frac{m}{16}$ **10.** $\frac{y}{3} = \frac{9}{27}$ **11.** $\frac{12}{y} = \frac{3}{5}$ **12.** $\frac{2}{7} = \frac{14}{x}$

13. $\frac{7}{15} = \frac{21}{c}$ **14.** $\frac{9}{r} = \frac{18}{24}$ **15.** $\frac{p}{5} = \frac{5}{25}$ **16.** $\frac{11}{2} = \frac{m}{8}$

Mathematics: Applications and Connections, Course 3

3-3 Practice

Solving Proportions

Determine whether each pair of ratios forms a proportion.

1. $\frac{8}{12}, \frac{12}{18}$

2. $\frac{4}{6}, \frac{5}{9}$

3. $\frac{5}{10}, \frac{6}{12}$

4. $\frac{8}{10}, \frac{12}{15}$

5. $\frac{9}{12}, \frac{12}{18}$

6. $\frac{15}{10}, \frac{9}{6}$

7. $\frac{28}{35}, \frac{8}{10}$

8. $\frac{16}{18}, \frac{24}{27}$

9. $\frac{5}{12}, \frac{7}{14}$

10. $\frac{16}{36}, \frac{24}{53}$

Solve each proportion.

11. $\frac{a}{3} = \frac{10}{15}$

12. $\frac{m}{4} = \frac{7}{14}$

13. $\frac{8}{14} = \frac{12}{y}$

14. $\frac{28}{35} = \frac{8}{w}$

15. $\frac{5}{10} = \frac{4}{n}$

16. $\frac{c}{21} = \frac{4}{6}$

17. $\frac{x}{13} = \frac{12}{26}$

18. $\frac{9}{d} = \frac{15}{40}$

19. $\frac{16}{20} = \frac{p}{15}$

20. $\frac{3}{7} = \frac{e}{4}$

21. $\frac{n}{85} = \frac{7}{119}$

22. $\frac{44}{72} = \frac{x}{108}$

3-4 Study Guide

Fractions, Decimals, and Percents

To express a percent as a decimal, divide by 100 and write as a decimal.

Examples   Express each percent as a fraction and as a decimal.

1 56%

$56\% = \frac{56}{100}$ or $\frac{14}{25}$

$56\% = 0.56$

2 3.4%

$3.4\% = \frac{3.4}{100}$ or $\frac{17}{500}$

$3.4\% = 0.034$

To express a decimal as a percent, first write the decimal as a fraction with a denominator of 100. Then write the fraction as a percent.

Examples   Express each decimal as a percent.

3 0.3

$0.3 = \frac{3}{10}$

$= 30\%$

4 0.17

$0.17 = \frac{17}{100}$

$= 17\%$

To express a fraction as a percent, you can use a proportion.

Examples   Express each fraction as a percent.

5 $\frac{7}{20}$

$\frac{7}{20} = \frac{n}{100}$

$20 \times n = 7 \times 100$

$20n = 700$

$n = 35$

6 $\frac{5}{12}$

$\frac{5}{12} = \frac{n}{100}$

$12 \times n = 5 \times 100$

$12n = 500$

$n \approx 41.7$

Express each percent as a decimal.

1. 45%   **2.** 91%   **3.** 24.5%   **4.** 8.37%

Express each decimal as a percent.

5. 0.13   **6.** 0.06   **7.** 0.765   **8.** 0.0122

Express each fraction as a percent.

9. $\frac{11}{50}$ **10.** $\frac{13}{20}$ **11.** $\frac{1}{8}$ **12.** $\frac{433}{1,000}$

3-4 Practice

Fractions, Decimals, and Percents

Express each percent as a decimal.

1. 8%

2. 32%

3. 15%

4. 15.7%

5. 16.23%

6. 2.01%

7. 3.2%

8. 80%

9. 1.32%

Express each decimal as a percent.

10. 0.21

11. 0.25

12. 0.13

13. 0.04

14. 0.4

15. 0.625

16. 0.3

17. 0.603

18. 0.123

Express each fraction as a percent.

19. $\frac{3}{20}$

20. $\frac{8}{25}$

21. $\frac{67}{100}$

22. $\frac{5}{8}$

23. $\frac{9}{50}$

24. $\frac{23}{100}$

25. $\frac{7}{10}$

26. $\frac{3}{200}$

27. $\frac{4}{125}$

Determine which is greater.

28. $\frac{1}{6}$ or 16%

29. 42% or $\frac{2}{5}$

30. $\frac{23}{10}$ or 23%

Mathematics: Applications and Connections, Course 3

3-5 Study Guide

Finding Percents

To find 1% of a number mentally, move the decimal point two places to the left. To find 10% of a number mentally, move the decimal point one place to the left.

Examples **1** **Find 1% of 19.5.**

$$1\% \text{ of } 19.5 = 0.19.5$$
$$= 0.195$$

2 **Find 10% of 0.39.**

$$10\% \text{ of } 0.39 = 0.0.39$$
$$= 0.039$$

To find the percent of a number, use common percents like 20%, 25%, or $33\frac{1}{3}\%$ whenever possible.

Examples **3** **Find 25% of 68.**

$$25\% \text{ of } 68 = \frac{1}{4} \times 68$$
$$= 17$$

4 **Find 60% of 125.**

$$60\% \text{ of } 125 = \frac{3}{5} \times 125$$
$$= 75$$

5 **Find 37.5% of 98.**

$$37.5\% \text{ of } 98 = \frac{3}{8} \times 98$$
$$= 36.75$$

6 **Find $33\frac{1}{3}\%$ of 57.**

$$33\frac{1}{3}\% \text{ of } 57 = \frac{1}{3} \times 57$$
$$= 19$$

Compute mentally.

1. 10% of 90

2. 1% of 62.5

3. 10% of 0.14

4. 20% of 75

5. 25% of 52

6. 50% of 18

7. 40% of 55

8. 60% of 10

9. 30% of 20

10. 12.5% of 56

11. $66\frac{2}{3}\%$ of 27

12. 37.5% of 72

3-5 Practice

Finding Percents

Compute mentally.

1. 1% of 127

2. 5% of 75

3. 50% of 84

4. 25% of 90

5. 37.5% of 64

6. $33\frac{1}{3}$% of 240

7. 20% of 95

8. 40% of 125

9. $66\frac{2}{3}$% of 150

10. 75% of 8

11. 60% of 120

12. $83\frac{1}{3}$% of 12

13. $12\frac{1}{2}$% of 88

14. 80% of 110

15. $16\frac{2}{3}$% of 90

16. 62.5% of 160

17. 30% of 40

18. 70% of 30

19. $87\frac{1}{2}$% of 320

20. 60% of 240

3-6 Study Guide

Percent and Estimation

You can use compatible numbers to estimate with percents.

Examples **1 Estimate 35% of 360.**

35% is about $\frac{1}{3}$. $\frac{1}{3}$ *and 360 are compatible numbers.*
$\frac{1}{3}$ of 360 is 120.

So, 35% of 360 is about 120.

2 Estimate 24% of 158.

24% is about $\frac{1}{4}$, and 158 is about 160. $\frac{1}{4}$ *and 160 are compatible numbers.*
$\frac{1}{4}$ of 160 is 40.

So, 24% of 158 is about 40.

3 Estimate 19 out of 48.

19 is about 20. 48 is about 50.
20 out of 50 is $\frac{2}{5}$ or 40%.

So, 19 out of 48 is about 40%.

Estimate the percent of the area shaded.

1.
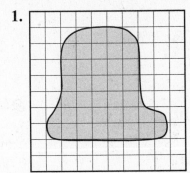

2.
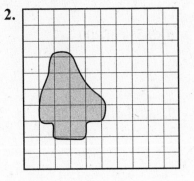

3.
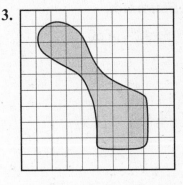

Estimate.

4. 52% of 240   **5.** 12% of 72   **6.** 65% of 270

7. 23% of 195   **8.** 42% of 309   **9.** 31% of 155

Estimate the percent.

10. 7 out of 15   **11.** 53 out of 77   **12.** 14 out of 112

13. 12 out of 98   **14.** 68 out of 208   **15.** 34 out of 140

Name _____ **Date** _____

3-6 Practice

Percent and Estimation

Estimate the percent of the area shaded.

1.
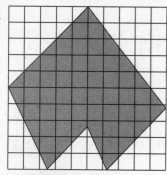

2.
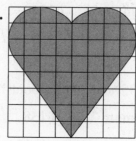

3.

4.
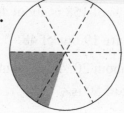

Estimate.

5. 48% of 50

6. 9.5% of 200

7. 76% of 12

8. 21% of 45

9. 35% of 36

10. 65% of 120

Estimate the percent.

11. 13 out of 60

12. 11 out of 80

13. 5 out of 26

14. 29 out of 119

15. 100 out of 102

16. 37 out of 80

Mathematics: Applications and Connections, Course 3

4-1 Study Guide

Bar Graphs and Histograms

A **bar graph** compares different categories of data by showing each as a bar whose length is related to the frequency.

Example 1   The table shows Americans' top five favorite snacks, by their share of total sales. Make a bar graph of the data.

Product	Share
Potato chips	31.9%
Tortilla chips	21.4%
Pretzels	8.6%
Snack nuts	8.4%
Popcorn	8.1%

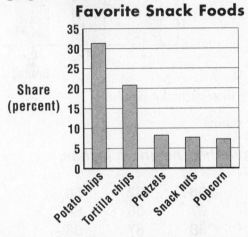

A **histogram** uses bars to display numerical data that have been organized into equal intervals.

Example 2   The table shows the percent of people in several age groups who are not covered by health insurance. Make a histogram of the data.

Age	Percent
under 18	12.4%
18-24	28.9%
25-34	20.9%
35-44	15.5%
45-54	14.0%
55-64	12.9%
over 65	1.2%

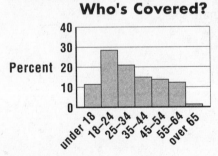

Make a histogram of the data below.

Pieces of Junk Mail	Frequency
0-4	25
5-9	35
10-14	50
15-19	40
20-24	15

Name _____ Date _____

4-1 Practice

Bar Graphs and Histograms

Use the bar graph at the right to answer each question.

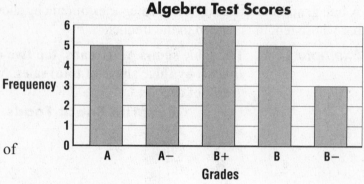

Algebra Test Scores

1. How many students took the algebra test?

2. Which grade has the most test scores?

3. Which grades have the same number of test scores?

4. How many more students earned a B+ than earned a B−?

5. Make a frequency table of the algebra scores.

A survey was taken that asked people their height in inches. The data are shown below.

68	69	72	64	74	56	62	58
69	65	70	59	71	67	66	64
73	78	70	52	61	68	67	66

6. Make a frequency table and histogram of the data. Use the intervals 51-55, 56-60, 61-65, 66-70, 71-75, and 76-80.

7. How many heights are in the 66-70 interval?

8. How many people in the survey are taller than 5 feet?

9. How many people in the survey are shorter than 5 feet?

10. What interval has the greatest number of heights?

11. How many people were surveyed?

Mathematics: Applications and Connections, Course 3

4-2 Study Guide

Circle Graphs

A **circle graph** shows how a whole is divided into parts.

The chassis of a race car cost $220,000. The engine cost $90,000. The tires and wheels cost $3,000. You can represent this data in a circle graph.

To make a circle graph for this data, first find the total cost of the race car: $220,000 + $90,000 + $3,000 = $313,000.

Then find the ratio that compares the cost of each of the parts to the total cost. Round to the nearest thousandth.

Chassis $220,000 \div 313,000 \approx 0.701$
Engine $90,000 \div 313,000 \approx 0.288$
Tires & Wheels $3,000 \div 313,000 \approx 0.01$

To find the number of degrees for each section, multiply each ratio by 360°. Round to the nearest degree.

Chassis $0.701 \times 360° = 252.36$ or 252
Engine $0.288 \times 360° = 103.68$ or 104
Tires & Wheels $0.01 \times 360° = 3.6$ or 4

Use a compass and protractor to construct a circle with angles at the center of 252°, 104°, and 4°.

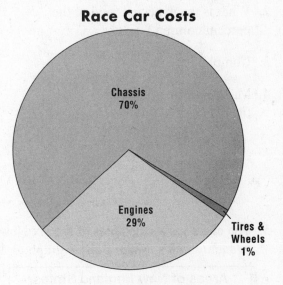

Race Car Costs

Make a circle graph of the data below.

Types of Human Bones	Number
Skull	29
Spine	26
Ribs and Breastbone	25
Shoulders, Arms and Hands	64
Pelvis, Legs, and Feet	62

4-2 Practice

Circle Graphs

Use the table at the right to answer Exercise 1-4.

1. What is the expected total of the degree column?

2. What is the expected total of the percent column?

3. Complete the table.

4. Make a circle graph of the data.

Monthly Budget			
Category	Amount	% of total	Degrees in graph
Housing	840		
Food	400		
Insurance	150		
Transportation	300		
Other	700		
TOTALS:			

5. The chart shows the areas of the six New England states in square miles. Make a circle graph to display the data.

Areas of New England States	
State	Area (square mi)
Maine	33,215
New Hampshire	9,304
Vermont	9,609
Massachusetts	8,257
Connecticut	5,009
Rhode Island	1,214

6. The chart shows the distribution of votes in New Hampshire in the 1988 presidential election. Make a circle graph to display the data.

N.H. 1988 Presidential Votes	
Party	No. of Votes
Republican	281,537
Democrat	163,692
Libertarian	4,502
Other	790

4-3 Study Guide

Line Plots

Another way to organize frequency data is with a line plot.

Example   **A restaurant owner asked her customers to rate the food on a scale of 0 (very bad) to 10 (very good). The data below shows the results. The meal at which the customer was surveyed is also shown: B = breakfast, L = lunch.**

5-B	7-L	9-L	0-B	6-B	6-L	8-B
10-L	4-B	8-L	8-B	2-B	8-L	7-B
4-B	7-B	7-L	6-B	9-L	10-L	6-B
7-B	5-B	9-L	8-L	7-L	6-B	3-B

For each customer, write the letter of the meal over the rating given.

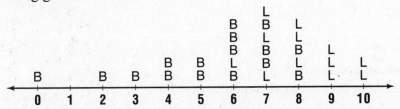

From the line plot, you can see that most ratings are between 6 and 8 and that lunch received better ratings than breakfast.

Movie goers were asked to rate a movie from 0 to 10. The rating and the age of the person responding were recorded: A = Adult, Y = Youth. Use the data to answer the questions.

7-A 8-A 5-Y 5-A 9-A 7-Y 6-Y 10-A 3-Y 6-Y 6-A
7-Y 8-A 2-Y 7-Y 5-A 6-Y 9-A 3-Y 8-Y 7-A 7-A

1. Make a line plot of the data.

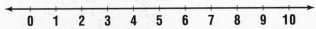

2. Analyze the line plot. Between what ratings does most of the data fall?

3. How are the ratings of adults different from the ratings of youths?

4-3 Practice

Line Plots

1. Make a line plot for the following scores.
   71, 74, 73, 71, 72, 74, 71, 75, 77, 79, 74, 72, 74, 75

2. The prices of appetizers are shown in the data list.
   $3.95, $6.95, $4.95, $3.95, $5.95, $3.95, $4.95, $3.95,
   $4.95, $4.95, $5.95, $4.95, $3.95, $4.95, $4.95, $5.95
   a. Make a line plot of the data.

   b. Which price is most common?
   c. How much does the most expensive appetizer cost?

3. Miss Allen asked her students during which half-hour they wake up
   regularly. She labeled the data with "M" for male and "F" for female.
   Use M's and F's to make a line plot of the data. Analyze your graph.
   5:30-M, 7:00-F, 6:30-F, 6:00-F, 6:30-M, 7:00-M, 6:30-F,
   7:00-M, 7:00-M, 6:30-M, 6:30-F, 7:30-F, 7:00-F, 6:30-M

4. The scores on a 60-point history test are listed below.
   55, 52, 49, 53, 38, 46, 52, 60, 55, 49, 32, 47, 55, 48, 60,
   51, 47, 44, 37, 51
   a. Make a line plot for the data.

   b. What are the highest and lowest scores?
   c. A passing score is 40. How many students passed the test?
   d. Which score occurred most often?

4-4 Study Guide

Measures of Central Tendency

Mean, median, and mode are three ways to measure the central tendency of a set of data.

Example   **Find the mean, median, and mode to the nearest tenth for the data shown on the line plot.**

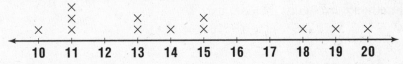

The **mean** is the sum of the data divided by the number of pieces of data.

$$\text{mean} = \frac{10 + 11 + 11 + 11 + 13 + 13 + 14 + 15 + 15 + 18 + 19 + 20}{12}$$

$$= 170 \div 12 \text{ or about } 14.2$$

The **median** is the number in the middle when the data are arranged in order. When there are two middle numbers, add them and divide by 2.

$$\text{median} = \frac{13 + 14}{2} = \frac{27}{2} \text{ or } 13.5$$

The **mode** is the number that appears most often. There may be one mode. There may be more than one mode. There may be no mode.

$$\text{mode} = 11$$

Find the mean, median and mode for each set of data. When necessary, round to the nearest tenth.

1. 6, 3, 8, 2, 5, 6, 4, 6, 9, 4

2. 15, 18, 34, 25, 10, 21, 16

3. 120, 145, 210, 175, 165, 120, 145

4. 15, 16, 37, 47, 2, 19, 22, 7, 5

5.

```
                    ×
  × ×  × ×          ×
                    ×      ×              ×
 ──┼──┼──┼──┼──┼──┼──┼──┼──┼──┼──┼──┼──┼──┼──
   30   34   38   42   46   50   54   58
     32   36   40   44   48   52   56
```

6.

```
          ×    ×
     ×    ×    ×    ×    ×
 ──┼────┼────┼────┼────┼────┼──
   15   16   17   18   19   20
```

Mathematics: Applications and Connections, Course 3

4-4 Practice

Measures of Central Tendency

Find the mean, median, and mode for each set of data. If necessary, round to the nearest tenth.

1. 2, 8, 3, 7, 5, 5, 7, 3, 5

2. 30, 37, 42, 44, 44, 46, 49, 52

3. 21, 27, 20, 29, 23, 21, 21, 27, 26, 25

4. 335, 428, 360, 480, 342

5. 6.42, 7.38, 5.29, 6.37, 6.9, 7.42, 5.3, 6.6

6. 4, 5, 5, 6, 6, 6, 6, 7

7. 2, 6, 10, 12, 8, 4

8. 13.6, 18.24, 16.7, 14.38, 15.29

9. 28, 32, 39, 25

10. 3, 3, 3, 9, 9, 4, 4, 4, 5

11. 29, 42, 44, 44, 45, 50, 51, 51, 52, 54, 58, 59, 61, 62, 63, 66, 71, 72

12.

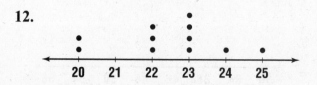

Mathematics: Applications and Connections, Course 3

4-5 Study Guide

Measures of Variation

The spread of a set of data is called the **variation.** One measure of variation is the **range.** The range of a set of data is the difference between the greatest and the least numbers in the set. Look at the data below.

30	32	34	36	37	41
44	45	48	48	48	49
50	51	52	53	55	

The least number is 30. The greatest number is 55. The range of the data is $55 - 30$ or 25.

The **interquartile range** is the range of the middle half of the data. To find the interquartile range, first find the median. The median of the data above is 48. Then find the **upper quartile** and **lower quartile** by finding the median of each half of the data.

lower quartile $= \frac{36 + 37}{2}$ or 36.5

upper quartile $= \frac{50 + 51}{2}$ or 50.5

The interquartile range is $50.5 - 36.5$ or 14.

Use the data in the list below to answer each question.

70	71	74	76	78	78	79
81	85	87	88	89	90	
93	96	96	97	97	98	

1. What is the range?

2. What is the median?

3. What are the upper and lower quartiles?

4. What is the interquartile range?

Use the data in the line plot.

5. What is the range?

6. What is the median?

7. What is the interquartile range?

4-5 Practice

Measures of Variation

Find the range, median, upper and lower quartiles, interquartile range, and any outliers for each set of data.

1. 8, 14, 32, 34, 36, 40

2. 43, 45, 56, 37, 11, 34

3. 9, 18, 3, 16, 22, 12, 15

4. 231, 428, 364, 229, 527, 683

5. 32, 20, 16, 36, 30, 18, 25

6. 53, 60, 66, 75, 54, 54, 46, 71, 51, 69, 62

7. 8, 12, 31, 20, 9, 21, 13, 33, 9, 22, 13, 14, 22, 24, 28

8. 26, 27, 28, 29, 30, 36, 37, 38, 39, 40, 41, 42, 43, 45, 50, 55, 58, 86

9. 28, 29, 29, 33, 34, 35, 37, 40, 42, 44, 46, 46, 47, 48, 53, 53, 54, 55, 55, 56, 57, 58, 59, 60, 61, 61, 62

10.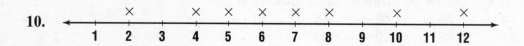

11.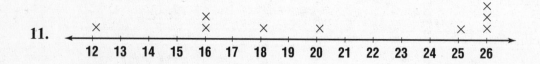

12. The data below represent the number of Indian reservations in the 34 states that have them.

1	1	1	1	1	1	1	1	1	1	1	1	2
3	3	3	3	3	4	4	4	4	7	7	8	8
9	11	14	19	23	25	27	96					

Name _____ **Date** _____

4-6 Study Guide

Integration: Algebra
Scatter Plots

When you graph two sets of data as ordered pairs, you make a **scatter plot**.
The pattern of the dots determines the relationship between the two sets of
data.

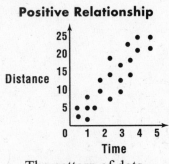

Positive Relationship

The pattern of dots
slants upward to
the right.

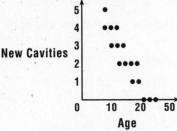

Negative Relationship

The pattern of dots
slants downward to
the right.

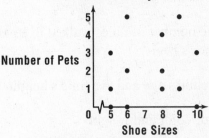

No Relationship

The dots are spread
out. There is no
pattern.

**Determine whether a scatter plot of the data below would show a
positive, negative, or no relationship.**

1. eye color and age

2. miles driven and gallons of gas used

3. driving speed and driving time

4. laps swum and swimming time

**The scatter plot shows the amount of time boys (B) and girls
(G) spent studying and their grades on a history test. Use the
scatter plot to answer the questions.**

5. Describe the relationship shown
by the scatter plot.

6. Is the relationship the same for
boys and for girls?

7. What other factors might affect the
grades on the history test?

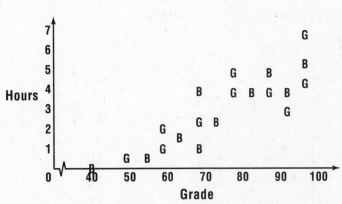

*Mathematics: Applications
and Connections,* Course 3

4-6 Practice

Integration: Algebra
Scatter Plots

Determine whether a scatter plot of the data below would show a positive, negative, or no relationship.

1. the selling price of a calculator and the number of functions it contains

2. the number of miles walked in a pair of shoes and the thickness of the shoe's heel

3. a child's age and the child's height

4. hair color and weight

5. number of minutes a candle burns and the candle's height

6. length of a taxi ride and the amount of the fare

7. gender and year of birth

8. height of a person and height of the person's second cousin

9. number of bank account and amount in bank-account balance

10. number of words written and amount of ink remaining in pen

11. number of letters in first name and height in centimeters

12. outside temperature and cost of air conditioning

Determine whether each scatter plot shows a positive, negative, or no relationship.

13.

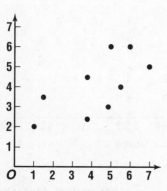

14.

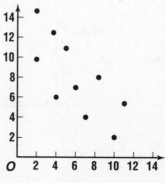

15.

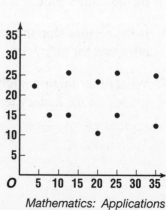

Mathematics: Applications and Connections, Course 3

4-7

Study Guide

Choosing an Appropriate Display

You are given data on the percentage of each age group in a recent survey that knew all 50 state capitals. What is the best way to display the data to show the differences between the age groups?

A circle graph is not appropriate. Circle graphs show how parts relate to the whole. A scatter plot is also not appropriate. Scatter plots illustrate the relationship between two variables.

Bar graphs and histograms are best used when showing a category on one axis and a frequency on the other axis. A histogram is most appropriate when the groups are organized in equal intervals. Thus, since these data would be divided into equal-sized age groups, a histogram would be the best choice.

Choose the most appropriate type of display for each data set and situation.

1. percentages of people who best like each of 5 different pizza toppings

2. ages and numbers of people who like in-line skating to determine marketing strategies for a brand of skates

3. age ranges of people who volunteer in America

4. total sales of the 8 best-selling soft drinks

5. amount of money spent on food, clothing, housing, and so on as compared to the monthly budget

6. numbers of different colors of candy in a package

7. number of telephones in homes surveyed for a newspaper article

8. number of people with 0, 1, 2, 3, 4, 5, . . . children

9. years and amount of the federal trade deficit for a report

10. prices of new 4-door sedans from 8 manufacturers to help you make a purchase

4-7 Practice

Choosing an Appropriate Display

Choose the most appropriate type of display for each data set and situation.

1. percentages of different kinds of juice sold in the United States

2. number of amateurs who play various musical instruments

3. number of evening meals American adults cook at home in an average week

4. market shares of all fast-food companies

5. year and number of cans recycled for a recycling industry report

6. percentage of college seniors' plans for five years in the future

7. cost of making each type of money (pennies, nickels, dimes, quarters, half-dollars, dollar bills)

8. sales of five best-selling albums of all time

9. composition of snack foods in a brand of party mix

10. attendance at top five theme parks for a year-end report

11. percentage of movie-goers who attend each month to show most popular month for move-going

12. age groups and allowances given

4-8 Study Guide

Misleading Graphs and Statistics

Graphs and statistics can be used to present data in ways that are misleading.

Examples

1 The scale does not begin at 0. The heights of the bars give the impression that twice as many people chose the Brand A as chose Brand B and that very few people chose Brand C.

2 Fifty 13- and 14-year-old students were surveyed. This sample is not representative of the entire population.

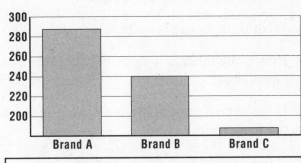

80% of the people surveyed believe that 14-year-olds should be allowed to drive!

Use the graph to answer the questions.

1. About how many times as many soccer balls did the uptown store sell as the downtown store?

2. How do the sizes of the soccer balls compare to the sales?

3. Is this a misleading graph? Explain.

Soccer Ball Sales

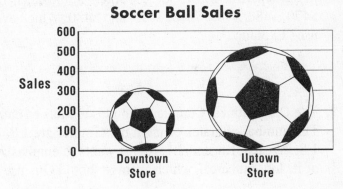

Decide whether each population is a representative sample for a survey.

Survey Topic	Population
4. best brand of baby food	mothers of children under age 3
5. longest wearing tires	junior high school students
6. best movie of the year	people entering a movie theater
7. best football team	people in San Francisco

Name_____ Date_____

4-8 | Practice

Misleading Graphs and Statistics

Look at the graph at the right.

1. What is the stock's price in April?

2. What is the stock's price in July?

3. How many times as long as the "July" bar is the "April" bar?

4. Is the "April" price of the stock twice as much as the "July" price?

Bank Stock Price

5. Is this a misleading graph? Explain.

6. John is offered a weekly salary that will be the average for the workers in his department. The seven workers in the department earn $480, $470, $480, $485, $490, $495, and $480. Which average should John use? Explain.

7. The Otis Oatmeal Company samples ten lots of oatmeal for fat content. The number of grams of fat in the samples are 1.8, 2.3, 2.2, 1.9, 2.0, 1.8, 1.7, 2.0, 1.8, and 2.1. If Otis wants to emphasize the health benefits of its low-fat cereal, which average should Otis use? Explain.

8. Soula has 11 stuffed animals, Maria has 12, and Nicole has 20 animals.
   a. Draw a bar graph that is not misleading.
   b. Draw a bar graph that makes it appear that Nicole has more than three times as many animals as Soula has.

33

5-1 Study Guide

Name _____ **Date** _____

Parallel Lines

Parallel lines are lines in the same plane that never intersect.
To say *line m is parallel to line n* we write $m \parallel n$.

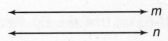

Example 1   **Name the parallel segments in the figure.**

$\overline{AB} \parallel \overline{ED}, \overline{BC} \parallel \overline{FE}, \overline{CD} \parallel \overline{AF}$

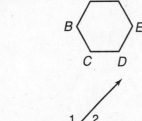

A line that intersects two or more lines is called a
transversal. If a pair of parallel lines is intersected
by a transversal, these pairs of angles are congruent.
The symbol ≅ means *is congruent to.*

alternate interior angles: $\angle 4 \cong \angle 6, \angle 3 \cong \angle 5$
alternate exterior angles: $\angle 1 \cong \angle 7, \angle 2 \cong \angle 8$
corresponding angles: $\angle 1 \cong \angle 5, \angle 2 \cong \angle 6,$
$\angle 3 \cong \angle 7, \angle 4 \cong \angle 8$

Example 2   **In the figure, $x \parallel y$. Find $m\angle 3$ if $m\angle 7 = 70°$.**

$\angle 3$ and $\angle 7$ are corresponding angles.
They are congruent, so their measures are the same.
$m\angle 3 = m\angle 7, m\angle 3 = 70°$
Find $m\angle 2$ if $m\angle 7 = 70°$.
$\angle 2$ and $\angle 7$ are alternate exterior angles.
They are congruent, so their measures are the same.
$m\angle 2 = m\angle 7, m\angle 2 = 70°$

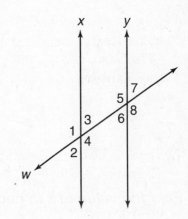

Name the parallel segments, if any, in each figure.

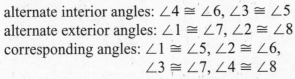

1. Q R T S

2. A B D C

3. H I M J L K

Use the figure at the right for Exercise 4-7. In the figure, $s \parallel t$.

4. Find $m\angle 2$ if $m\angle 6 = 75°$.

5. Find $m\angle 5$ if $m\angle 3 = 105°$.

6. Find $m\angle 8$ if $m\angle 3 = 105°$.

7. Find $m\angle 4$ if $m\angle 6 = 75°$.

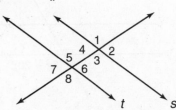

5-1 Practice

Parallel Lines

If ℓ ∥ m, use the figure at the right for Exercises 1-3.

1. Find $m\angle 1$, if $m\angle 3 = 57°$.

2. Find $m\angle 4$, if $m\angle 5 = 136°$.

3. Find $m\angle 2$, if $m\angle 7 = 113°$.

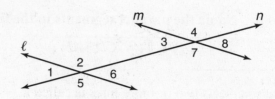

Find the value of each variable in the figure at the right if p ∥ q and h = 130°.

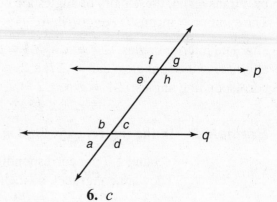

4. a 5. b 6. c

7. d 8. e 9. f

10. g

Find the value of x in each figure if a ∥ b.

11.

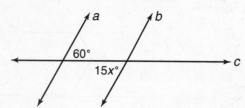

12.

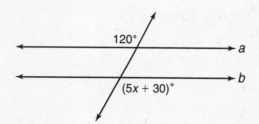

Mathematics: Applications and Connections, Course 3

5-2 **Study Guide**

Name_____ Date_____

Classifying Triangles

Triangles may be classified by the lengths of their sides or by the measures of their angles.

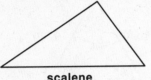

scalene

All sides are
different lengths.

isosceles

Two sides are the
same length.

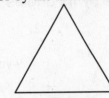

equilateral

All three sides are the
same length.

acute

All three angles
are acute.

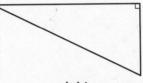

right

One angle is a right angle.
The symbol └ shows a right
angle.

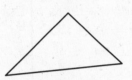

obtuse

One angle is an
obtuse angle.

Classify each triangle by its angles and by its sides.

1.

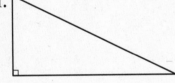

2.

3.

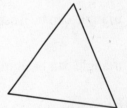

4.

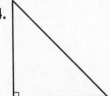

5.

6.

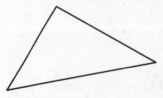

Tell whether each statement is true or false. Then draw a figure to justify your answer.

7. A right triangle can never be isosceles.

8. A triangle can be right and equilateral.

© Glencoe/McGraw-Hill

35

*Mathematics: Applications
and Connections,* Course 3

5-2 Practice

Classifying Triangles

Classify each triangle by its angles and by its sides.

1.

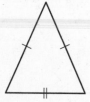

15.6 ft
9 ft
30°
60°
18 ft

2.

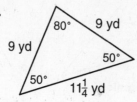

80° 9 yd
9 yd
50°
50°
$11\frac{1}{4}$ yd

3.

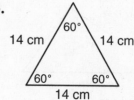

60°
14 cm   14 cm
60°   60°
14 cm

4.

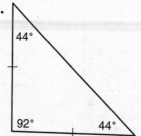

5.

44°
92°   44°

5.

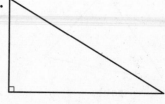

Tell whether each statement is true or false. Then draw a figure to justify your answer.

7. A triangle can be isosceles and right.

8. A triangle can be obtuse and equilateral.

9. A triangle can be scalene and acute.

10. A right triangle can be an obtuse triangle.

11. An equilateral triangle is acute.

12. A triangle can contain two right angles.

13. Find the value of x in $\triangle ABC$ if $m\angle A = 94°$, $m\angle B = 47°$, and $m\angle C = x°$.

14. Find the value of x in $\triangle WYZ$ if $m\angle W = 37°$, $m\angle Y = 68°$, and $m\angle Z = 5x°$.

Study Guide

Classifying Quadrilaterals

A **quadrilateral** is a figure with four sides and four angles. You can use
sides and angles to classify quadrilaterals.

Parallelogram   Opposite sides are parallel.
                      Opposite sides are congruent.

Trapezoid   One pair of parallel sides.

Rectangle   Opposite sides are parallel.
                      Opposite sides are congruent.
                      All four angles are right angles.

Rhombus   Opposite sides are parallel.
                      All four sides are congruent.

Square   Opposite sides are parallel.
                      All four sides are congruent.
                      All four angles are right angles.

Example   **Identify all names that describe each quadrilateral.**

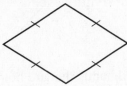
quadrilateral
parallelogram
rectangle
rhombus
square

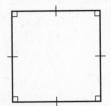
quadrilateral
parallelogram
rhombus

Let Q = quadrilateral, P = parallelogram, R = rectangle,
S = square, RH = rhombus, and T = trapezoid. Write all of the
letters that describe the figure inside it.

1.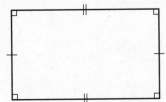

2.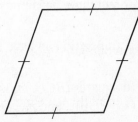

3.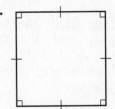

4.

5.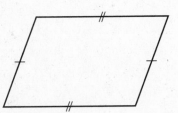

6.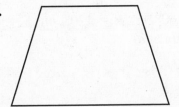

5-3 Practice

Classifying Quadrilaterals

Let Q = quadrilateral, P = parallelogram, R = rectangle, S = square, RH = rhombus, and T = trapezoid. Write all of the letters inside the figure that describe it.

1.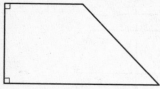

2.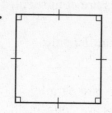

3.

4.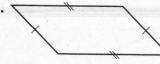

5.

6.

7.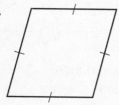

8.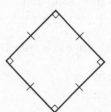

9.

10. Name all of the quadrilaterals that are both a rhombus and a rectangle.

Tell whether each statement is true or false. Then draw a figure to justify your answer.

11. A rectangle has opposite sides congruent.

12. A trapezoid can have three right angles.

13. In square $ABCD$, $m\angle A = 3x°$, $m\angle B = (x + 60)°$, $m\angle C = (4x - 30)°$, and $m\angle D = (2x + 30)°$. Find the value of x.

14. In trapezoid $QRST$, $m\angle Q = 60°$, $m\angle R = 120°$, $m\angle S = 113°$, and $m\angle T = a°$. Find the value of a.

Mathematics: Applications and Connections, Course 3

5-4 Study Guide

Symmetry

If you can fold a figure along a line so that the two parts reflect each other, the figure has a line of symmetry.

Examples   one line of symmetry   three lines of symmetry   no lines of symmetry

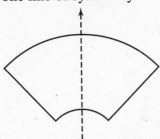
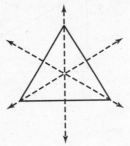
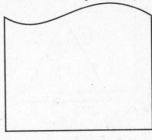

A figure has rotational symmetry if it can be turned less than 360° about its center and it looks like the original figure.

Example   Original   72° turn   144° turn   216° turn   288° turn

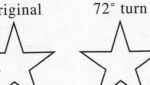

Draw the line(s) of reflection for each figure.

1.   2.   3.   4.

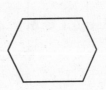
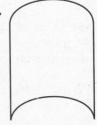

Determine whether each figure has rotational symmetry.

5.   6.   7.   8.

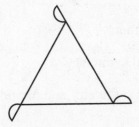

37   *Mathematics: Applications and Connections*, Course 3

Name_____ Date_____

5-4 Practice

Symmetry

Determine whether each figure has line symmetry. If so, draw the line(s) of reflection.

1.
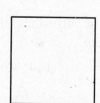

2.
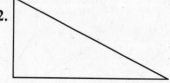

3.
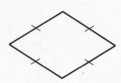

4.
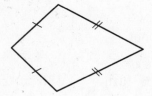

5.
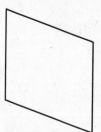

6.

7. Which of the figures above have rotational symmetry?

Determine whether each figure has rotational symmetry.

8.
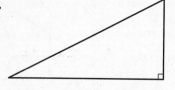

9.
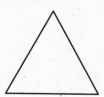

10.
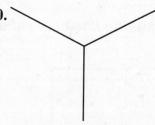

11. Draw an isosceles triangle.

    a. Does an isosceles triangle have line symmetry?

    b. Does an isosceles triangle have rotational symmetry?

12. What classification of triangle has both line symmetry and rotational symmetry?

Name _____ Date _____

Study Guide

Congruent Triangles

If two figures are exactly the same size and shape, they are **congruent**.
Two triangles are congruent if the following corresponding parts of two
triangles are congruent.

- three sides (SSS)
- two angles and the included side (ASA)
- two sides and the included angle (SAS)

Example **Determine whether the triangles are congruent. If so, write a
congruence statement and tell why the triangles are congruent.**

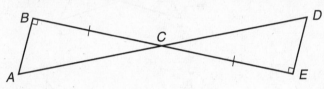

$\overline{BC} \cong \overline{CE}$
$\angle ACB \cong \angle DCE$ by vertical angles.
Since $\angle B$ and $\angle E$ are right angles, $\angle B \cong \angle E$.
Therefore, $\triangle ABC \cong \triangle CDE$ by ASA.

**Determine whether each set of triangles is congruent. If so, write a
congruence statement and tell why the triangles are congruent.**

1.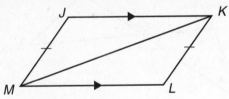

2.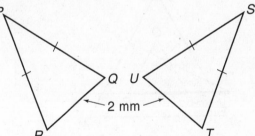

Find the value of x in each pair of congruent triangles.

3.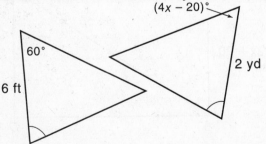

4.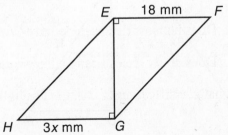

*Mathematics: Applications
and Connections, Course 3*

Name_____ **Date**_____

Practice

Congruent Triangles

Determine whether each set of triangles is congruent. If so, write
a congruence statement and tell why the triangles are congruent.

1.
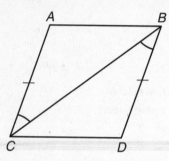

2.
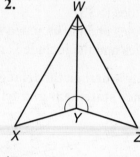

3.
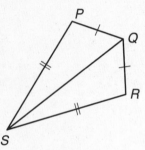

4.
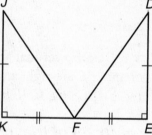

5.
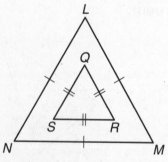

6.
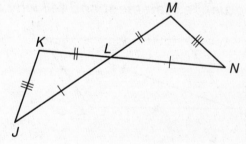

Find the value of x in each pair of congruent triangles.

7.
8.
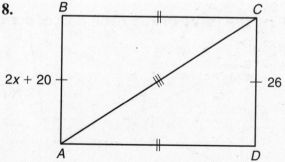

© Glencoe/McGraw-Hill

38

*Mathematics: Applications
and Connections, Course 3*

Name _____ Date _____

5-6   Study Guide

Similar Triangles

Triangles that have the same shape, but may differ in size are called
similar triangles. If corresponding angles are congruent and
corresponding sides are proportional, then the triangles are similar.

Example   **Determine whether the triangles are similar. Justify
your answer.**

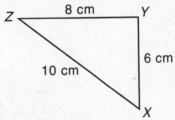

Corresponding angles are congruent.
Corresponding sides are proportional.

$$\frac{AB}{XY} = \frac{3}{6} \text{ or } \frac{1}{2} \qquad \frac{BC}{YZ} = \frac{4}{8} \text{ or } \frac{1}{2} \qquad \frac{AC}{XZ} = \frac{5}{10} \text{ or } \frac{1}{2}$$

Therefore, the triangles are similar.

*Tell whether each pair of triangles is congruent, similar, or
neither. Justify your answer.*

1.
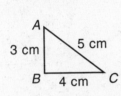

2.
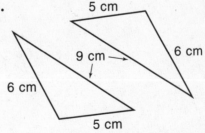

3.
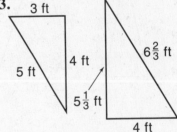

4.
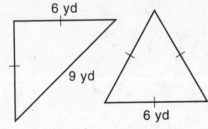

5.
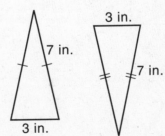

6.
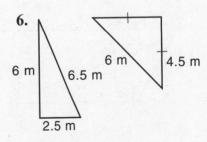

*Mathematics: Applications
and Connections, Course 3*

Name _____ **Date** _____

5-6 Practice

Similar Triangles

Tell whether each pair of triangles is congruent, similar, or neither. Justify your answer.

1.

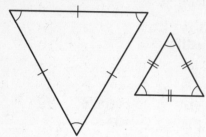

2.

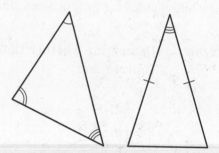

3.

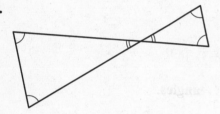

4.

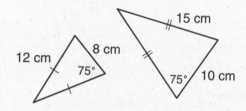

5.

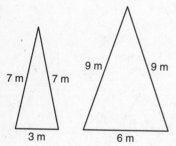

6.

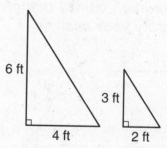

7.

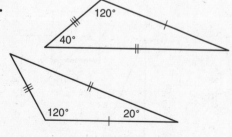

8.

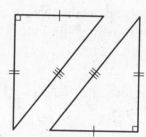

© Glencoe/McGraw-Hill

39

Mathematics: Applications and Connections, Course 3

5-7 Study Guide

Transformations and M.C. Escher

M.C. Escher (1898-1972) was a Dutch artist famous for his repetitive interlocking patterns. You can use transformations to create Escher-like patterns.

Slides and rotations are examples of **transformations.**

Example 1   **Use slides to modify a tessellation of squares.**

Tessellation of squares

Make a change on the top of the square. Slide the change to the bottom of the square.

Make a change on one side of the square. Slide the change to the other side of the square.

Repeat the pattern.

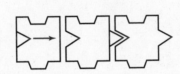
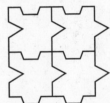

Example 2   **Use a rotation to modify a tessellation of triangles.**

Tessellation of triangles

Change one side.

Rotate the triangle. Copy the change.

Repeat the pattern.

Make an Escher-like drawing for each pattern described. For squares, use a tessellation of two rows of three squares as the base. For the triangle, use a tessellation of two rows of five equilateral triangles as the base.

1.

2.

3.

5-7 **Practice**

Transformations and M.C. Escher

Make an Escher-like drawing for each pattern described. Use a tessellation of two rows of three squares as your base.

1.

2.

3.

4. Tell whether each pattern in Exercises 1-3 involves a translation or a rotation.

Make an Escher-like drawing for each pattern described. For the square, use a tessellation of two rows of three squares as your base. For the triangle, use a tessellation of two rows of five equilateral triangles as your base.

5.

6.

6-1 Study Guide

Divisibility Patterns

The following rules will help you determine if a number is divisible by
2, 3, 4, 5, 6, 8, 9, or 10.

A number is divisible by:

- 2 if the ones digit is divisible by 2.
- 3 if the sum of the digits is divisible by 3.
- 4 if the number formed by the last two digits is divisible by 4.
- 5 if the ones digit is 0 or 5.
- 6 if the number is divisible by 2 and 3.
- 8 if the number formed by the last three digits is divisible by 8.
- 9 if the sum of the digits is divisible by 9.
- 10 if the ones digit is 0.

Example **Determine whether 2,120 is divisible by 2, 3, 4, 5, 6, 9, or 10.**

2: The ones digit is divisible by 2.
2,120 is divisible by 2.

3: The sum of the digits 2 + 1 + 2 + 0 = 5, is not divisible by 3.
2,120 is not divisible by 3.

4: The number formed by the last two digits, 20, is divisible by 4.
2,120 is divisible by 4.

5: The ones digit is 0.
2,120 is divisible by 5.

6: The number is divisible by 2 but not by 3.
2,120 is not divisible by 6.

8: The number formed by the last 3 digits, 120, is divisible by 8.
2,120 is divisible by 8.

9: The sum of the digits, 2 + 1 + 2 + 0 = 5, is not divisible by 9.
2,120 is not divisible by 9.

10: The ones digit is 0.
2,120 is divisible by 10.
2,120 is divisible by 2, 4, 5, 8, and 10.

**Determine whether the first number is divisible by the second
number. Write yes or no.**

1. 4,829; 9   2. 482; 2   3. 1,692; 6

4. 1,355; 10   5. 633; 3   6. 724; 4

7. 3,714; 8   8. 912; 9   9. 559; 5

10. 20,454; 6   11. 616; 8   12. 3,000; 4

6-1 Practice

Divisibility Patterns

Determine whether each number is divisible by 2, 3, 4, 5, 6, 8, 9, or 10.

1. 80

2. 91

3. 180

4. 333

5. 1,024

6. 11,010

7. Is 9 a factor of 154?

8. Is 6 a factor of 102?

9. Is 486 divisible by 6?

10. Is 441 divisible by 9?

Determine whether the first number is divisible by the second number.

11. 4,281; 2

12. 2,670; 10

13. 3,945; 6

14. 6,132; 4

15. 8,304; 3

16. 6,201; 9

17. 4,517; 9

18. 2,304; 8

19. 7,000; 5

20. 10,000; 8

21. 9,420; 6

22. 822; 4

Use mental math to find a number that satisfies the given conditions.

23. a number divisible by both 3 and 5

24. a four-digit number divisible by 3, but *not* by 9

25. a five-digit number *not* divisible by 3 or 10

26. a four-digit number divisible by 2 and 4, but *not* by 8

Mathematics: Applications and Connections, Course 3

Name_____   Date_____

6-2 Study Guide

Prime Factorization

A whole number greater than 1 with exactly two factors, 1 and itself, is called a **prime number.**

Example 1 19 is a prime number. It has only 1 and 19 as factors.

A whole number greater than 1 with more than two factors is called a **composite number.**

Example 2 18 is a composite number. It has 1, 2, 3, 6, 9, and 18 as factors.

The numbers 0 and 1 are neither prime nor composite.

A composite number may be written as the product of prime numbers. This product is the **prime factorization** of the number.

Example 3 **Find the prime factorization of 660.**

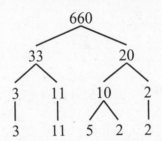

Write the number as the product of two factors.

Continue to factor until only prime factors remain.

The prime factorization of 660 is $3 \cdot 11 \cdot 5 \cdot 2 \cdot 2$.

Determine whether each number is prime, composite, or neither.

1. 28

2. 47

3. 39

4. 61

5. 53

6. 0

7. 159

8. 1

Find the prime factorization of each number.

9. 30

10. 155

11. 169

12. 100

13. 86

14. 98

15. 495

16. 40

Mathematics: Applications and Connections, Course 3

6-2 Practice

Prime Factorization

Determine whether each number is prime, composite, or neither.

1. 81

2. 47

3. 61

4. 32

5. 23

6. 57

7. 17

8. 27

9. 0

10. 1,331

11. 1

12. 613

Find the prime factorization of each number.

13. 60

14. 420

15. 128

16. 88

17. 96

18. 400

19. 93

20. 150

21. 84

22. 2,000

23. 1,760

24. 15,840

6-3 Study Guide

Greatest Common Factor

The greatest of the factors common to two or more number is the **greatest common factor (GCF).** One way to find the GCF is to list all of the factors of each number. Then find the greatest number that is in both lists.

Example 1 **Find the GCF of 32 and 48.**

Factors of 32: 1, 2, 4, 8, 16, 32
Factors of 48: 1, 2, 3, 4, 6, 8, 12, 16, 24, 48

The common factors of 32 and 48 are 1, 2, 4, 8, and 16.
The greatest common factor of 32 and 48 is 16.

You can use prime factorization to find the greatest common factor.

Example 2 **Find the greatest common factor of 90 and 120.**

$$90 = 3 \cdot 30$$
$$= 3 \cdot 15 \cdot 2$$
$$= 3 \cdot 5 \cdot 3 \cdot 2$$

$$120 = 3 \cdot 40$$
$$= 3 \cdot 10 \cdot 4$$
$$= 3 \cdot 2 \cdot 5 \cdot 2 \cdot 2$$

90 and 120 have 2, 3, and 5 as common factors.
The product of the common factors is the greatest common factor.
$2 \cdot 3 \cdot 5 = 30$
30 is the greatest common factor of 90 and 120.

Find the GCF of each set of numbers.

1. 24, 40

2. 18, 30

3. 12, 48

4. 36, 90

5. 50, 20

6. 15, 17

7. 52, 16

8. 63, 42

9. 25, 40

10. 36, 12, 72

11. 28, 49, 105

12. 30, 45, 75

Mathematics: Applications and Connections, Course 3

Greatest Common Factor

Find the GCF of each set of numbers.

1. $6 = 2 \cdot 3$
   $15 = 3 \cdot 5$

2. $12 = 2 \cdot 2 \cdot 3$
   $18 = 2 \cdot 3 \cdot 3$

3. $20 = 2 \cdot 2 \cdot 5$
   $60 = 2 \cdot 2 \cdot 3 \cdot 5$

4. $40 = 2 \cdot 2 \cdot 2 \cdot 5$
   $35 = 5 \cdot 7$

5. $22 = 2 \cdot 11$
   $33 = 3 \cdot 11$

6. $16 = 2 \cdot 2 \cdot 2 \cdot 2$
   $24 = 2 \cdot 2 \cdot 2 \cdot 3$
   $36 = 2 \cdot 2 \cdot 3 \cdot 3$

7. 24, 36

8. 80, 120

9. 45, 60

10. 45, 56

11. 26, 65

12. 96, 88

13. 50, 75

14. 48, 72

15. 66, 79

16. 24, 30, 40

17. 100, 200, 350

18. 510, 680, 850

19. How do you know just by looking that two numbers will have 2 as a common factor?

20. What is the GCF of $2^3 \cdot 3^2 \cdot 5$ and $2^2 \cdot 3^2 \cdot 5^3$?

21. What is the GCF of $2 \cdot 3 \cdot 11$ and $3^2 \cdot 17$?

6-4 Study Guide

Rational Numbers

Whole numbers are numbers in the set {0, 1, 2, 3, . . .}. **Integers** are the whole numbers and their opposites.

Rational numbers are numbers that can be expressed in the form $\frac{a}{b}$, where a and b are integers and $b \neq 0$.

Examples $6\frac{1}{7}$ can be written as $\frac{43}{7}$.   58 can be written as $\frac{58}{1}$.

0.65 can be written as $\frac{65}{100}$. -79 can be written as $-\frac{79}{1}$.

-0.7 can be written as $-\frac{7}{10}$.   0 can be written as $\frac{0}{1}$.

When a rational number is expressed as a fraction, it is commonly written in simplest form. A fraction is in simplest form when the GCF of the numerator and denominator is 1.

Example   **Write $\frac{18}{24}$ in simplest form.**

Method 1   Divide by the GCF.
$18 = 2 \cdot 3 \cdot 3$
$24 = 2 \cdot 2 \cdot 2 \cdot 3$
The GCF is $2 \cdot 3 = 6$.

Method 2   Use prime factorization.
$\frac{18}{24} = \frac{\cancel{2} \cdot \cancel{3} \cdot 3}{\cancel{2} \cdot 2 \cdot 2 \cdot \cancel{3}} = \frac{3}{4}$

The slashes show that the numerator and denominator are divided by $2 \cdot 3$, the GCF.

Since the GCF of 3 and 4 is 1, the fraction $\frac{3}{4}$ is in simplest form.

Name all sets of numbers to which each number belongs.

1. $4\frac{1}{2}$

2. 14.5

3. 17

4. 0.78

Write each fraction in simplest form.

5. $\frac{16}{26}$

6. $\frac{24}{72}$

7. $\frac{36}{78}$

8. $\frac{21}{56}$

9. $\frac{30}{75}$

10. $\frac{20}{48}$

11. $\frac{45}{81}$

12. $\frac{28}{49}$

6-4 Practice

Rational Numbers

Name all the sets of numbers to which each number belongs.

1. $\frac{2}{3}$

2. -1.7

3. -3

4. $\frac{200}{5}$

5. 0

6. $-\frac{6}{2}$

7. 9

8. $6\frac{2}{5}$

9. 4.7

Write each fraction in simplest form.

10. $\frac{8}{24}$

11. $\frac{15}{60}$

12. $\frac{27}{36}$

13. $-\frac{42}{50}$

14. $-\frac{32}{48}$

15. $-\frac{18}{37}$

16. $\frac{18}{36}$

17. $-\frac{24}{45}$

18. $\frac{64}{72}$

19. $\frac{18}{22}$

20. $\frac{32}{70}$

21. $\frac{17}{52}$

22. $\frac{15}{80}$

23. $-\frac{68}{17}$

24. $\frac{36}{104}$

25. $-\frac{24}{100}$

26. $\frac{18}{54}$

27. $-\frac{30}{75}$

28. $\frac{1,000}{2,000}$

29. $\frac{14}{64}$

30. $-\frac{9}{108}$

6-5 Study Guide

Rational Numbers and Decimals

To change a fraction to a decimal, divide the numerator by the denominator.

Example 1 **Express $\frac{5}{8}$ as a decimal.**

Use a calculator.

5 $\boxed{\div}$ 8 $\boxed{=}$ *0.625*

$\frac{5}{8} = 0.625$

The remainder is 0.
0.625 is a terminating decimal.

Use paper and pencil.

$$\begin{array}{r} 0.625 \\ 8)\overline{5.000} \\ -48 \\ \hline 20 \\ -16 \\ \hline 40 \\ -40 \\ \hline 0 \end{array}$$

Annex zeros as needed.

$\frac{5}{8} = 0.625$

A **terminating decimal** can be written as a fraction with a denominator of 10, 100, 1000, and so on.

Examples **Express each decimal as a fraction or mixed number in simplest form.**

2 $0.52 = \frac{52}{100}$

$= \frac{13}{25}$

3 $-1.4375 = -1\frac{4375}{10,000}$

$= -1\frac{7}{16}$

Express each fraction as a decimal.

1. $\frac{3}{5}$ 2. $-\frac{7}{10}$ 3. $-\frac{7}{4}$ 4. $-\frac{15}{32}$ 5. $\frac{3}{20}$

6. $5\frac{7}{25}$ 7. $-\frac{24}{16}$ 8. $-6\frac{3}{8}$ 9. $\frac{14}{35}$ 10. $\frac{5}{40}$

Express each decimal as a fraction or mixed number in simplest form.

11. 0.08   12. -3.75 13. 0.015   14. -0.6 15. 1.05

16. -12.34 17. 2.1875   18. -0.875 19. -8.85 20. 9.5

Mathematics: Applications and Connections, Course 3

6-5 Practice

Rational Numbers and Decimals

Express each decimal using bar notation.

1. $-37.888888\ldots$

2. $0.233333\ldots$

3. $4.56565656\ldots$

4. $54.545454\ldots$

5. $1.1234234\ldots$

6. $-2.0020202\ldots$

Write the first ten decimal places of each decimal.

7. $0.4\overline{7}$

8. $0.\overline{36}$

9. $0.2\overline{48}$

10. $3.1\overline{9}$

11. $0.31\overline{9}$

12. $0.2\overline{040}$

Express each fraction or mixed number as a decimal.

13. $-\frac{3}{5}$

14. $2\frac{5}{8}$

15. $\frac{17}{4}$

16. $-\frac{9}{20}$

17. $\frac{31}{40}$

18. $-\frac{7}{32}$

Express each decimal as a fraction or mixed number in simplest form.

19. 5.95

20. 7.075

21. -4.875

22. 12.12

23. 6.92

24. -4.5625

25. $0.\overline{5}$

26. $1.\overline{45}$

27. $-0.\overline{02}$

Mathematics: Applications and Connections, Course 3

6-6 Study Guide

Integration: Probability
Simple Events

If you toss a coin, there are two possible outcomes, heads or tails. Each outcome has the same chance of occurring. The two outcomes are equally likely. A particular outcome, such as tossing a tail, or a set of outcomes is an event. **Probability** is the chance that an event will happen.

$$\text{Probability} = \frac{\text{number of ways an event can occur}}{\text{number of possible outcomes}}$$

Tossing tails can occur 1 way out of 2 possible outcomes, So, $P(\text{tail}) = \frac{1}{2}$.

The probability of an event can be written as a number from 0 to 1. If it is impossible for an event to happen, the event has a probability of 0. If an event is certain to happen, it has a probability of 1.

Impossible   Equal chance   Certain

0 $\frac{1}{2}$

Example   **Maryanne writes the letters in her name on tennis balls, one letter per ball. If she puts the balls in a bag and draws one without looking, find each probability.**

$P(m) = \frac{1}{8}$ or 0.125 $P(\text{vowel}) = \frac{3}{8}$ or 0.375

$P(\text{not } a) = \frac{6}{8}$ or 0.75 $P(w) = \frac{0}{8}$ or 0

$P(a \text{ or } n) = \frac{4}{8}$ or 0.5 $P(m, a, r, y, n, \text{ or } e) = \frac{8}{8}$ or 1

A box contains 6 black crayons, 4 blue crayons, 5 red crayons, 3 yellow crayons, and 2 white crayons. If one crayon is chosen without looking, find the probability of each event.

1. $P(\text{black})$ **2.** $P(\text{blue})$ **3.** $P(\text{not white})$ **4.** $P(\text{pink})$

5. $P(\text{black or blue})$ **6.** $P(\text{red, yellow, or white})$

The numbers from 1 to 25 are written on slips of paper and one is drawn without looking. Find the probability of each event.

7. $P(\text{an odd number})$ **8.** $P(\text{a three digit number})$ **9.** $P(\text{not } 4)$

10. $P(\text{a positive number})$ **11.** $P(\text{a prime number})$ **12.** $P(> 19)$

6-6 Practice

Integration: Probability
Simple Events

State the probability of each outcome as a fraction and as a decimal.

1. A die is rolled, and it shows a number divisible by 2.

2. Tomorrow, the sun will rise in the west.

3. Two coins are tossed, and both coins show heads.

4. You will be older tomorrow than you are now.

5. A whole number chosen between 5 and 10 will be 7.

A bag contains two black, eight red, five orange, and five green jelly beans. A blindfolded student draws one jelly bean. Find the probability of each outcome.

6. It is not black.

7. It is orange.

8. It is black or red.

9. It is blue.

10. It is not yellow.

11. It is red, green, or black.

The letters of the word "commutative" are written, one each on 11 identical slips of paper, and shuffled in a hat. A blindfolded student draws one slip of paper. Find each probability.

12. $P(t)$

13. $P(\text{not } i)$

14. $P(n)$

15. $P(\text{vowel})$

16. $P(s \text{ or } v)$

17. $P(\text{not } s \text{ or } a)$

Numbers from 1 to 30 are printed on table-tennis balls, mixed by a machine, and drawn at random. One ball is drawn.

18. What is $P(\text{an odd number})$?

19. What is $P(\text{a one-digit number})$?

20. What is $P(\text{a negative number})$?

21. What is $P(\text{a perfect square})$?

22. What is $P(\text{a number divisible by 8})$?

23. What is $P(\text{a two-digit number})$?

24. What is $P(\text{a number greater than 17 but less than 26})$?

6-7

Study Guide

Least Common Multiple

A multiple of a number is the product of that number and any whole number. The least nonzero multiple of two or more numbers is the **least common multiple (LCM)** of the numbers.

Example 1   **Find the least common multiple of 12 and 15.**

multiples of 12: 0, 12, 24, 36, 48, 60, 72, 84, 96, 108, 120, 132, . . .
multiples of 15: 0, 15, 30, 45, 60, 75, 90, 105, 120, 135, . . .
60 and 120 are common multiples. The LCM is 60.

Prime factorization can also be used to find the LCM.

Example 2   **Find the least common multiple of 15, 28, and 30.**

$15 = 3 \cdot 5$ *Find the prime factors of each number.*
$28 = 2 \cdot 2 \cdot 7$
$30 = 2 \cdot 3 \cdot 5$

2, 3, 5   *Find the common factors.*

$2 \cdot 3 \cdot 5 \cdot 2 \cdot 7 = 420$ *Multiply the common factors and any other factors.*

The LCM of 15, 28, and 30 is 420.

Find the LCM of each set of numbers.

1. 9, 15

2. 16, 12

3. 42, 12

4. 6, 10

5. 21, 15

6. 15, 20

7. 9, 15, 18

8. 4, 10, 8

9. 12, 15, 24

10. 30, 21, 7

11. 13, 52, 24

12. 8, 14, 28

6-7 Practice

Least Common Multiple

List the first six multiples of each number or algebraic expression.

1. 8

2. 25

3. x

Find the LCM for each set of numbers.

4. 2, 4, 5

5. 5, 6, 18

6. 12, 16, 30

7. 12, 16

8. 5, 10, 20

9. 18, 30, 50

10. 14, 22

11. 6, 8, 10

12. 12, 20

13. 9, 15, 12

14. 6, 8, 36

15. 24, 16, 30

16. 13, 5, 17

17. 24, 16, 9

18. 15, 20, 30

19. 12, 25, 18

20. 36, 80, 75

21. 8, 52, 65

22. 14, 21, 35

23. 24, 36, 48

24. 15, 18, 24

25. 6, 16, 26

26. 150, 375

27. 111, 112

6-8 Study Guide

Comparing and Ordering Rational Numbers

One way to compare rational numbers is to express them as fractions with like denominators.

Example 1 Replace $\bigcirc$ with $<$, $>$, or $=$ to make $\frac{6}{7} \bigcirc \frac{7}{9}$ a true sentence.

Method 1 Use fractions.

The least common denominator (LCD) of 7 and 9 is 63.

$$\frac{6}{7} \overset{\times 9}{=} \frac{54}{63} \qquad \frac{7}{9} \overset{\times 7}{=} \frac{49}{63}$$

$\frac{54}{63} > \frac{49}{63}$; so $\frac{6}{7} > \frac{7}{9}$.

Method 2 Use decimals.

$6 \div 7 = 0.857142857$

$7 \div 9 = 0.7777777778$

$0.857 > 0.778$, so $\frac{6}{7} > \frac{7}{9}$.

Another way to compare rational numbers is to express them as decimals. Then compare the decimals.

Example 2 Order $\frac{4}{9}, \frac{2}{5}, 0.\overline{47}$, and 0.45 from least to greatest.

$\frac{4}{9} = 4 \div 9$ or $0.\overline{4}$ $\frac{2}{5} = 2 \div 5$ or 0.4

The rational numbers in order from least to greatest are:

$\frac{2}{5}, \frac{4}{9}, 0.45, 0.\overline{47}$.

Replace each $\bigcirc$ with $<$, $>$, or $=$ to make a true sentence.

1. $3.7 \bigcirc 3.\overline{7}$

2. $\frac{5}{8} \bigcirc \frac{7}{11}$

3. $-6.8 \bigcirc -6\frac{4}{5}$

4. $0.555 \bigcirc \frac{5}{9}$

5. $6\frac{7}{12} \bigcirc 6.6$

6. $\frac{3}{10} \bigcirc \frac{5}{16}$

Order each set of rational numbers from least to greatest.

7. $0.67, 0.6, 0.7, 0.06$

8. $\frac{3}{7}, \frac{2}{5}, \frac{5}{8}, \frac{1}{2}$

9. $-\frac{1}{3}, \frac{7}{8}, -\frac{9}{10}, \frac{13}{14}$

10. $\frac{15}{13}, 1.2, \frac{19}{18}$

11. $-\frac{1}{6}, \frac{1}{6}, -\frac{2}{15}, \frac{1}{9}$

12. $1.77, 1\frac{5}{6}, 1\frac{1}{2}, 1.46$

6-8 Practice

Comparing and Ordering Rational Numbers

Find the LCD for each pair of fractions.

1. $\frac{7}{9}, \frac{5}{12}$

2. $\frac{3}{10}, \frac{4}{15}$

3. $-\frac{3}{10}, \frac{5}{6}$

Replace each $\bigcirc$ with <, >, or = to make a true statement.

4. $-11.6 \bigcirc 10.7$

5. $3.234 \bigcirc 3.243$

6. $3\frac{3}{5} \bigcirc 3.6$

7. $0.\overline{6} \bigcirc 0.666$

8. $0.312 \bigcirc 0.313$

9. $-4.27 \bigcirc -4.28$

10. $3\frac{1}{5} \bigcirc 3\frac{1}{3}$

11. $2.99 \bigcirc 2.\overline{98}$

12. $\frac{16}{3} \bigcirc 5.\overline{3}$

13. $\frac{1}{7} \bigcirc \frac{4}{21}$

14. $1.001 \bigcirc 1.0001$

15. $0.09 \bigcirc 0.\overline{1}$

16. $2\frac{2}{9} \bigcirc 2\frac{4}{18}$

17. $\frac{17}{51} \bigcirc 0.\overline{3}$

18. $-6.\overline{1} \bigcirc 6.08$

Order each set of rational numbers from least to greatest.

19. $2, -3, 4, -5, 6$

20. $1, 1.1, 1.01, 1.\overline{11}$

21. $2, -2, -2.1, 2.\overline{1}$

22. $\frac{2}{3}, \frac{1}{2}, \frac{3}{5}$

23. $0, -2.1, \frac{3}{2}, \frac{2}{3}$

24. $\frac{4}{11}, 0.35, 0.3\overline{6}$

25. $\frac{3}{4}, \frac{9}{10}, \frac{7}{8}, \frac{2}{3}$

26. $-0.3, -\frac{1}{3}, -0.33, -0.35$

Mathematics: Applications and Connections, Course 3

6-9 Study Guide

Scientific Notation

A number in **scientific notation** is written as the product of a number between 1 and 10 and a power of ten.

Examples

1 **Express 8.65×10^7 in standard form.**

$8.65 \times 10^7 = 8.65 \times 10,000,000$

$\qquad\qquad = 8.6500000.$ *Move the decimal point 7 places to the right.*

$\qquad\qquad = 86,500,000$

2 **Express 9.1×10^{-4} in standard form.**

$9.1 \times 10^{-4} = 9.1 \times \frac{1}{10^4}$

$\qquad\qquad = 9.1 \times \frac{1}{10,000}$

$\qquad\qquad = 9.1 \times 0.0001$

$\qquad\qquad = 0.0009.1$ *Move the decimal point 4 places to the left.*

$\qquad\qquad = 0.00091$

3 **Express 1,088,000 in scientific notation.**

1.088000.   *Move the decimal point to the right of the first nonzero digit. Move the decimal point 6 places to the left.*

$1,088,000 = 1.088 \times 10^6$

4 **Express 0.0000762 in scientific notation.**

0.00007.62   *Move the decimal point to the right of the first nonzero digit. Move the decimal point 5 places to the right.*

$0.0000762 = 7.62 \times 10^{-5}$

Express each number in standard form.

1. 7.02×10^4 **2.** 1.1×10^{-3} **3.** 6.4×10^7

4. 5.9×10^8 **5.** 9.12×10^{-2} **6.** 8.8×10^{-5}

Express each number in scientific notation.

7. 0.0003   **8.** 4,600,000   **9.** 0.00001653

10. 518,900,000   **11.** 720   **12.** 0.114

6-9 Practice

Scientific Notation

Express each number in standard form.

1. 4.2×10^6

2. 3.75×10^2

3. -8.45×10^7

4. -6.32×10^{-5}

5. 8.84×10^{-7}

6. 4.125×10^5

7. 3.72×10^{-6}

8. -6.1×10^8

9. -3.4×10^{-3}

10. 3.45×10^6

11. 2.2846×10^7

12. 3.45×10^{-4}

Express each number in scientific notation.

13. 0.01624

14. 1,200

15. 0.00000008

16. 4,862

17. 9,000,000

18. 0.000023

19. 0.000603

20. 42,000,000

21. 423,000

22. 1,100,000,000

23. 0.0000061

24. 0.00412

25. 3,250,000

26. 32,500,000,000

27. 0.143

Name_____ Date_____

Study Guide

Adding and Subtracting Like Fractions

To add fractions with like denominators, add the numerators.

Examples   **1**   Solve $m = \frac{7}{8} + \left(-\frac{5}{8}\right)$.

$m = \frac{2}{8}$ *Add the numerators.*

$m = \frac{1}{4}$ *Simplify.*

2   Solve $n = \frac{5}{6} + \frac{5}{6}$.

$n = \frac{10}{6}$ *Add the numerators.*

$n = 1\frac{4}{6}$ *Rename the improper fraction as a mixed number.*

$n = 1\frac{2}{3}$ *Simplify.*

To subtract fractions with like denominators, subtract the numerators.

Examples   **3**   Solve $a = \frac{8}{9} - \frac{5}{9}$.

$a = \frac{3}{9}$ *Subtract the numerators.*

$a = \frac{1}{3}$ *Simplify*

4   Solve $b = -\frac{5}{8} - \left(-\frac{3}{8}\right)$.

$b = -\frac{2}{8}$ *Subtract the numerators.*

$b = -\frac{1}{4}$ *Simplify.*

Solve each equation. Write the solution in simplest form.

1. $\frac{4}{7} + \frac{2}{7} = f$

2. $\frac{3}{4} - \frac{1}{4} = p$

3. $a = \frac{5}{8} + \frac{5}{8}$

4. $z = -\frac{2}{3} + \frac{1}{3}$

5. $-\frac{5}{12} - \frac{1}{12} = t$

6. $v = -\frac{6}{11} + \left(-\frac{5}{11}\right)$

7. $-\frac{1}{8} - \left(-\frac{3}{8}\right) = k$

8. $\frac{14}{15} + \frac{6}{15} = x$

9. $c = -\frac{1}{2} - \frac{1}{2}$

10. $j = -\frac{12}{13} + \frac{5}{13}$

11. $-\frac{13}{16} + \left(-\frac{11}{16}\right) = k$

12. $r = -\frac{2}{3} - \left(-\frac{2}{3}\right)$

Mathematics: Applications and Connections, Course 3

7-1 Practice

Adding and Subtracting Like Fractions

Solve each equation. Write the solution in simplest form.

1. $a = \frac{2}{7} + \frac{1}{7}$

2. $\frac{9}{5} - \frac{6}{5} = x$

3. $w = -\frac{5}{12} - \frac{7}{12}$

4. $b = -\frac{3}{4} - \frac{1}{4}$

5. $-\frac{4}{7} - \left(-\frac{6}{7}\right) = y$

6. $2\frac{3}{4} + 5\frac{3}{4} = q$

7. $t = -\frac{6}{7} + \left(-\frac{3}{7}\right)$

8. $-4\frac{1}{9} - 2\frac{7}{9} = f$

9. $d = -\frac{5}{13} + \left(-\frac{7}{13}\right)$

10. $j = -2\frac{4}{9} - \frac{4}{9}$

11. $\frac{3}{8} - \left(-\frac{5}{8}\right) = p$

12. $h = \frac{7}{12} - \left(-\frac{1}{12}\right)$

13. Find the sum of $\frac{5}{9}$ and $-\frac{2}{9}$.

14. Subtract $-\frac{3}{11}$ from $-\frac{1}{11}$.

Evaluate each expression if a = $-\frac{2}{7}$, b = $\frac{15}{7}$ and c = $-\frac{5}{7}$.

15. $a + b$

16. $b - a$

17. $a - b$

18. $a - c$

19. $b - c$

20. $a + b + c$

7-2 Study Guide

Adding and Subtracting Unlike Fractions

To add or subtract fractions or mixed numbers with unlike denominators, rename the fractions with a common denominator. Then add or subtract.

Examples

1 Solve $a = -\frac{5}{8} + \left(-\frac{3}{4}\right).$ *The least common denominator of 8 and 4 is 8.*

$a = -\frac{5}{8} + \left(-\frac{6}{8}\right)$ *Rename $-\frac{3}{4}$ as $-\frac{6}{8}$.*

$a = -\frac{11}{8}$ *Add.*

$a = -1\frac{3}{8}$ *Rename the improper fraction as a mixed number.*

2 Solve $c = -2\frac{3}{5} - 1\frac{1}{2}.$ *The least common denominator of 5 and 12 is 10.*

$c = -2\frac{6}{10} - 1\frac{5}{10}$ *Rename $\frac{3}{5}$ as $\frac{6}{10}$. Rename $\frac{1}{2}$ as $\frac{5}{10}$.*

$c = -3\frac{11}{10}$ *Subtract.*

$c = -4\frac{1}{10}$ *Rename $\frac{11}{10}$ as $1\frac{1}{10}$.*

3 Solve $r = 5\frac{1}{4} - 2\frac{2}{3}.$ *The least common denominator of 4 and 3 is 12.*

$r = 5\frac{3}{12} - 2\frac{8}{12}$ *Rename $\frac{1}{4}$ as $\frac{3}{12}$. Rename $\frac{2}{3}$ as $\frac{8}{12}$.*

$r = 4\frac{15}{12} - 2\frac{8}{12}$ *Rename $5\frac{3}{12}$ as $4\frac{15}{12}$.*

$r = 2\frac{7}{12}$ *Subtract.*

Solve each equation. Write the solution in simplest form.

1. $n = \frac{3}{4} + \frac{1}{3}$

2. $\frac{7}{8} - \frac{2}{3} = k$

3. $-\frac{11}{12} - \frac{1}{2} = y$

4. $1\frac{1}{2} + \left(-1\frac{1}{5}\right) = v$

5. $x = -3\frac{2}{3} + \left(-1\frac{1}{6}\right)$

6. $m = 10\frac{11}{12} + 9\frac{3}{8}$

7. $p = 7\frac{1}{3} - \left(-2\frac{5}{9}\right)$

8. $-\frac{15}{16} - \frac{3}{8} = f$

9. $3\frac{4}{5} - \left(-5\frac{1}{2}\right) = c$

10. $2\frac{3}{4} + \left(-6\frac{3}{8}\right) = a$

11. $-9\frac{5}{6} - \left(-3\frac{2}{3}\right) = q$

12. $m = \frac{5}{9} - \frac{1}{3}$

Mathematics: Applications and Connections, Course 3

7-2 Practice

Adding and Subtracting Unlike Fractions

Complete.

1. $4\frac{3}{7} = 3\frac{\square}{7}$

2. $8\frac{2}{3} = 7\frac{\square}{3}$

3. $2\frac{4}{9} = 1\frac{\square}{9}$

Solve each equation. Write the solution in simplest form.

4. $a = \frac{2}{3} + \frac{7}{12}$

5. $r = -\frac{5}{12} + \frac{3}{8}$

6. $-\frac{3}{10} + \left(-\frac{2}{5}\right) = x$

7. $2\frac{2}{3} + \left(-4\frac{1}{4}\right) = q$

8. $4\frac{3}{4} - \left(-2\frac{3}{8}\right) = g$

9. $t = \frac{11}{12} - 1\frac{2}{3}$

10. $-3\frac{3}{5} - \frac{9}{10} = b$

11. $-2\frac{1}{5} - 3\frac{3}{4} = s$

12. $-2\frac{1}{3} - \left(-4\frac{4}{6}\right) = d$

13. $p = 8 - 3\frac{2}{3}$

14. $c = 3\frac{2}{3} - 8$

15. $w = -10\frac{2}{9} - \left(-3\frac{1}{3}\right)$

16. Find the sum of $\frac{4}{9}$ and $\frac{5}{27}$.

17. What is $3\frac{2}{3}$ less than $-5\frac{1}{12}$?

Evaluate each expression if $x = \frac{3}{8}$, $y = 2\frac{7}{12}$, **and** $z = -\frac{5}{6}$.

18. $x + y + z$

19. $x - z$

20. $y - (-z)$

21. $x + z$

22. $y - x$

23. $z + (-y)$

7-3 Study Guide

Multiplying Fractions

To multiply fractions, multiply the numerators and multiply the denominators. Use the rules for multiplying integers when you multiply negative fractions.

Example 1 Solve $k = -\frac{4}{7} \times \frac{5}{9}$.

$k = -\frac{4 \times 5}{7 \times 9}$ *Multiply the numerators.*
Multiply the denominators.

$k = -\frac{20}{63}$ *The product of two rational numbers with different signs is negative.*

Example 2 Solve $n = 3\frac{1}{3} \times 2\frac{1}{5}$.

$n = \frac{\overset{2}{\cancel{10}}}{3} \times \frac{11}{\underset{1}{\cancel{5}}}$ *Rename $3\frac{1}{3}$ as $\frac{10}{3}$. Rename $2\frac{1}{5}$ as $\frac{11}{5}$.*
The GCF of 10 and 5 is 5. Divide 10 and 5 by 5.

$n = \frac{2 \times 11}{3 \times 1} = \frac{22}{3}$ *Multiply the numerators.*
Multiply the denominators.

$n = 7\frac{1}{3}$ *Simplify.*

Solve each equation. Write the solution in simplest form.

1. $k = \frac{2}{3} \times \frac{3}{5}$

2. $-\frac{1}{2} \times \frac{7}{9} = m$

3. $-\frac{4}{7} \times \left(-\frac{7}{8}\right) = n$

4. $1\frac{1}{2} \times 1\frac{2}{3} = v$

5. $x = -2\frac{1}{4} \times \frac{2}{9}$

6. $r = -8 \times \left(-\frac{3}{4}\right)$

7. $p = \frac{3}{8} \times \left(-2\frac{2}{3}\right)$

8. $6\frac{1}{2} \times \frac{4}{5} = w$

9. $9 \times \left(-2\frac{2}{3}\right) = h$

10. $4\left(5\frac{3}{4}\right) = f$

11. $c = \left(\frac{1}{2}\right)^2$

12. $t = \frac{4}{7} \times \left(-\frac{2}{3}\right)$

Mathematics: Applications and Connections, Course 3

7-3 Practice

Multiplying Fractions

Solve each equation. Write the solution in simplest form.

1. $b = \frac{3}{8} \cdot \frac{8}{11}$

2. $\frac{4}{7} \cdot \frac{11}{20} = h$

3. $d = \frac{3}{5} \cdot 4$

4. $-5\frac{1}{3}\left(-\frac{2}{3}\right) = a$

5. $-4\left(\frac{5}{8}\right) = q$

6. $s = 7\frac{1}{3} \cdot \frac{6}{11}$

7. $j = 4\frac{1}{2} \cdot 3\frac{1}{4}$

8. $g = -2\frac{1}{4}\left(-\frac{1}{3}\right)$

9. $6\left(-5\frac{2}{3}\right) = r$

10. $t = \frac{1}{6} \cdot 1\frac{2}{5}$

11. $p = 6\frac{1}{6} \cdot \left(-\frac{6}{37}\right)$

12. $(-6)\left(3\frac{1}{3}\right) = k$

13. $8\frac{2}{3} \cdot 3\frac{1}{2} = f$

14. $\left(2\frac{1}{2}\right)\left(-3\frac{1}{3}\right) = c$

15. $w = 4\left(-\frac{3}{10}\right)$

Evaluate each expression if $b = \frac{2}{3}$, $c = -2\frac{3}{4}$, $t = \frac{1}{5}$, and $w = -1\frac{1}{2}$.

16. w^2

17. $t^2(-c)$

18. $2b$

19. cw

20. bc

21. tw

22. bct

23. c^2

24. btw

25. ctw

26. bcw

27. t^2w^2

Mathematics: Applications
and Connections, Course 3

7-4

Study Guide

Properties of Rational Numbers

Use the basic properties for addition and multiplication of rational numbers to help you evaluate expressions.

Commutative Property

For any numbers a and b:
$a + b = b + a$
$a \times b = b \times a$

Associative Property

For any numbers a, b, and c:
$(a + b) + c = a + (b + c)$
$(a \times b) \times c = a \times (b \times c)$

Identity Property

For any number a:
$a + 0 = a$
$a \times 1 = a$

Examples

$\frac{1}{4} + \frac{2}{3} = \frac{2}{3} + \frac{1}{4}$

$\frac{4}{5} \times \frac{1}{2} = \frac{1}{2} \times \frac{4}{5}$

Examples

$\left(-\frac{1}{3} + \frac{2}{5}\right) + \frac{1}{2} = -\frac{1}{3} + \left(\frac{2}{5} + \frac{1}{2}\right)$

$\left(\frac{5}{7} \times -\frac{3}{4}\right) \times \frac{1}{3} = \frac{5}{7} \times \left(-\frac{3}{4} \times \frac{1}{3}\right)$

Examples

$\frac{7}{8} + 0 = \frac{7}{8}$

$-\frac{11}{12} \times 1 = -\frac{11}{12}$

Distributive Property

For any numbers a, b, and c:

$a \times (b + c) = (a \times b) + (a \times c)$

Inverse Property of Multiplication

For any numbers a and b, with $a, b \neq 0$:

$\frac{a}{b} \times \frac{b}{a} = 1$

Example

$4 \times \left(7 + \frac{5}{8}\right) = \left(4 \times 7\right) + \left(4 \times \frac{5}{8}\right)$

Example

$\frac{2}{5} \times \frac{5}{2} = 1$ $\frac{2}{5}$ and $\frac{5}{2}$ are reciprocals or multiplicative inverses of each other.

Name the multiplicative inverse of each rational number.

1. 8

2. -7

3. $\frac{3}{4}$

4. $-\frac{9}{15}$

5. 0.5

6. $\frac{r}{t}$

7. $-p$

8. $2\frac{1}{4}$

9. $-\frac{m}{n}$

10. k

Evaluate each expression if $a = \frac{1}{4}$, $b = \frac{3}{8}$, $x = -1\frac{1}{2}$, and $y = 2\frac{2}{3}$.

11. ab

12. $2x$

13. by

14. a^2

7-4 Practice

Properties of Rational Numbers

Name the multiplicative inverse of each rational number.

1. 4

2. $-\frac{1}{5}$

3. $3\frac{4}{7}$

4. -1

5. -0.8

6. 2.1

Solve each equation using properties of rational numbers.

7. $k = 6\left(3\frac{1}{2}\right)$

8. $\frac{1}{2} \cdot 8\frac{6}{7} = m$

9. $n = \frac{1}{2} \cdot \left(-\frac{8}{9}\right)$

10. $b = \frac{3}{4} \cdot \left(-\frac{4}{3}\right)$

11. $w = \left(-\frac{6}{5}\right)\left(3\frac{3}{5}\right)$

12. $\frac{3}{5} \cdot 1\frac{2}{3} = y$

Evaluate each expression if $m = -\frac{2}{3}$, $n = \frac{1}{2}$, $s = -3\frac{3}{4}$, and $t = 2\frac{1}{6}$.

13. $6m$

14. nt

15. m^2

16. $st - m$

17. $2m - 3n$

18. $n^2(t + 2)$

7-5 Study Guide

Integration: Patterns and Functions
Sequences

A list of numbers in a specific order is a **sequence.** Each number is called a **term** of the sequence. When the difference between any two consecutive terms is the same, the sequence is an **arithmetic sequence.**

Examples
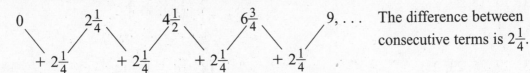
The difference between consecutive terms is $2\frac{1}{4}$.

When consecutive terms are formed by multiplying by the same factor, the sequence is **geometric.**

Example
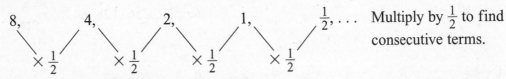
Multiply by $\frac{1}{2}$ to find consecutive terms.

Some sequences are neither arithmetic or geometric.

Example
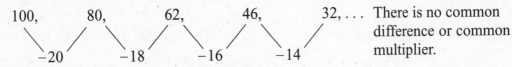
There is no common difference or common multiplier.

Identify each sequence as arithmetic, geometric, or neither. Then write the next three terms.

1. 47, 42, 37, 32, . . .

2. 9, 18, 36, 72, . . .

3. $\frac{1}{9}, \frac{1}{3}, 1, 3, 9, \ldots$

4. 15, 17, 20, 24, 29, . . .

5. $8, 7\frac{3}{5}, 7\frac{1}{5}, 6\frac{4}{5}, \ldots$

6. $8, 2, \frac{1}{2}, \frac{1}{8}, \ldots$

7. $-9, -5, -1, 3, 7, \ldots$

8. $\frac{4}{7}, \frac{2}{7}, 0, -\frac{2}{7}, \ldots$

9. 1, 1, 2, 3, 5, 8, . . .

10. $\frac{1}{10}, \frac{1}{2}, 2\frac{1}{2}, 12\frac{1}{2}, \ldots$

7-5 Practice

Integration: Patterns and Functions
Sequences

**Identify each sequence as arithmetic, geometric, or neither.
Then find the next three terms.**

1. 13, 18, 23, 28, . . .

2. $\frac{1}{2}, \frac{1}{3}, \frac{1}{4}, \frac{1}{5}, \ldots$

3. 27, 25, 23, 21, . . .

14. 16, −15, 14, −13, . . .

5. 3, 6, 12, 24, . . .

6. 512, 256, 128, 64, . . .

7. 1, 2, 4, 7, . . .

8. 7, −7, 7, −7, . . .

9. 1, −4, 16, −64, . . .

10. 1.3, 2.6, 3.9, 5.2, . . .

11. 8, 8, 8, 8, . . .

12. 20, 18, 15, 13, 10, . . .

Write the next three terms of each sequence.

13. 17, 34, 51, 68, . . .

14. 216, 36, 6, 1, . . .

15. 8, 12, 18, 27, . . .

16. 8, 0, 8, 0, . . .

17. −2, 4, −6, 8, . . .

18. 17, 23, 29, 35, . . .

19. The sixth term of an arithmetic sequence is 50. The common
   difference is −3. Find the second term of the sequence.

20. Name the ninth term in the sequence 17, 22, 27, ...

7-6 Study Guide

Integration: Geometry
Area of Triangles and Trapezoids

The area of a triangle is equal to one-half its base times its height: $A = \frac{1}{2}bh$.

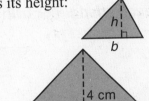

Example 1 Find the area of the triangle.

$A = \frac{1}{2}bh$.

$A = \frac{1}{2}(7.5)(4)$ $b = 7.5, h = 4$

$A = 2(7.5)$

$A = 15$ The area is 15 square centimeters.

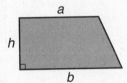

The area of a trapezoid is equal to one-half its height times the sum of its bases: $A = \frac{1}{2}h(a + b)$.

Example 2 Find the area of the trapezoid.

$A = \frac{1}{2}h(a + b)$

$A = \frac{1}{2}(6)\left(10\frac{1}{2} + 14\frac{1}{2}\right)$ $h = 6, a = 10\frac{1}{2}, b = 14\frac{1}{2}$

$A = 3(25)$

$A = 75$ The area is 75 square inches.

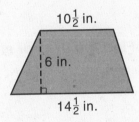

State the measures of the base(s) and the height of each triangle or trapezoid. Then find the area of each figure.

1.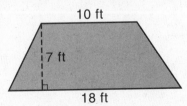

2.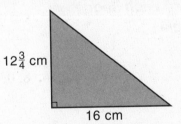

3.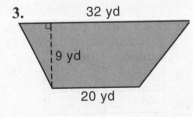

4.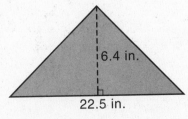

5.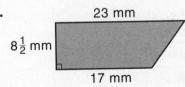

6.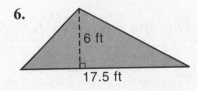

Mathematics: Applications and Connections, Course 3

7-6 Practice

Integration: Geometry
Area of Triangles and Trapezoids

Find the area of each triangle or trapezoid.

1.
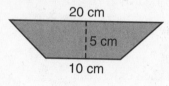
40 ft
60 ft

2.
20 cm
5 cm
10 cm
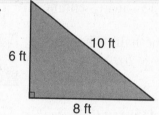

3.
20 m
30 m
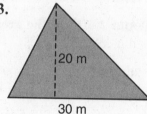

4.
20 cm
30 cm
18 cm
16 cm
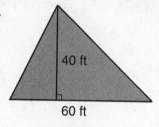

5.
10 ft
6 ft
8 ft
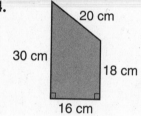

6.
7 ft
13 ft 12 ft 13 ft
17 ft
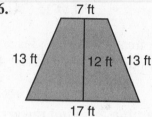

Find the area of each figure.

7. triangle: base 16.4 cm; height, 18.8 cm

8. trapezoid: bases, 3.2 ft and 3.4 ft; height, 2.6 ft

Find the area of each triangle.

	base	height
9.	1.6 cm	1.5 cm
10.	46 ft	28 ft

Find the area of each trapezoid.

	base (a)	base (b)	height
11.	16 ft	22 ft	14 ft
12.	12.4 cm	18.6 cm	10.2 cm

*Mathematics: Applications
and Connections, Course 3*

Name_____ Date_____

Study Guide

Integration: Geometry
Circles and Circumference

A **circle** is a set of points in a plane that are the same distance from a given point called the **center.**

The **diameter** (*d*) is the distance across the circle through its center.

The **radius** (*r*) is the distance from the center to any point on the circle.

The **circumference** (*C*) is the distance around the circle.

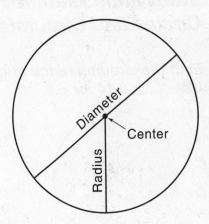

Examples

1 **Find the circumference of a circle with a diameter of 9.5 inches.**

$C = \pi d$
$C = 3.14 \times 9.5$ *Use 3.14 for π.*
$C \approx 29.83$
The circumference of the circle is about 29.83 inches.

2 **Find the circumference of a circle with a radius of 14 inches.**

$C = 2\pi r$
$C = 2 \times \frac{22}{7} \times 14$ *Use $\frac{22}{7}$ for π.*
$C \approx 88$
The circumference of the circle is approximately 88 inches.

Find the circumference of each circle to the nearest tenth.
Use $\frac{22}{7}$ or 3.14 for π.

1.

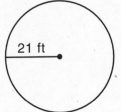

21 ft

2.

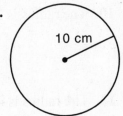

10 cm

3.

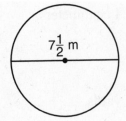

$7\frac{1}{2}$ m

4.

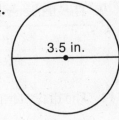

3.5 in.

5. The radius is 42 miles.

6. The diameter is 68 meters.

7. The diameter is 700 feet.

8. The radius is $7\frac{3}{4}$ inches.

9. The radius is 91 centimeters.

10. The diameter is $2\frac{1}{3}$ kilometers.

Mathematics: Applications and Connections, Course 3

7-7 **Practice**

Integration: Geometry
Circles and Circumference

Find the circumference of each circle to the nearest tenth.
Use $\frac{22}{7}$ or 3.14 for π.

1.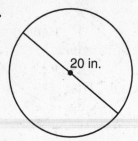
20 in.

2.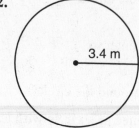
3.4 m

3.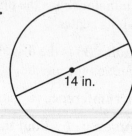
14 in.

4.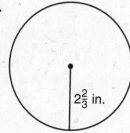
$2\frac{2}{3}$ in.

5.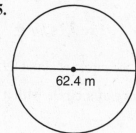
62.4 m

6.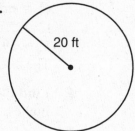
20 ft

7. The diameter is $4\frac{1}{7}$ inches.

8. The radius is 18 feet.

9. The diameter is 36.4 centimeters.

10. The radius is 27 yards.

11. The diameter is $6\frac{2}{3}$ yards.

12. The radius is 4.9 feet.

13. The diameter is $2\frac{1}{2}$ miles.

14. The diameter is 6.8 meters.

7-8 Study Guide

Dividing Fractions

To divide by a fraction, multiply by its multiplicative inverse. Use the rules
for dividing integers when you divide negative fractions.

Examples **1** Solve $m = 24 \div \frac{3}{4}$.

$m = \frac{24}{1} \div \frac{3}{4}$ *Rename 24 as $\frac{24}{1}$.*

$m = \frac{24}{1} \times \frac{4}{3}$ *Multiply by $\frac{4}{3}$, the multiplicative inverse of $\frac{3}{4}$.*

$m = 32$

2 Solve $p = -2\frac{1}{3} \div \frac{5}{6}$.

$p = -\frac{7}{3} \div \frac{5}{6}$ *Rename $-2\frac{1}{3}$ as $-\frac{7}{3}$.*

$p = -\frac{7}{3} \times \frac{6}{5}$ *Multiply by $\frac{6}{5}$, the multiplicative inverse of $\frac{5}{6}$.*

$p = -\frac{14}{5}$ *The product of a negative number and a positive number is negative.*

$p = -2\frac{4}{5}$ *Rename $-\frac{14}{5}$ as $-2\frac{4}{5}$.*

3 Solve $r = -\frac{7}{8} \div \left(-4\frac{1}{2}\right)$.

$r = -\frac{7}{8} \div \left(-\frac{9}{2}\right)$ *Rename $-4\frac{1}{2}$ as $-\frac{9}{2}$.*

$r = -\frac{7}{8} \times \left(-\frac{2}{9}\right)$ *Multiply by $-\frac{2}{9}$, the multiplicative inverse of $-\frac{9}{2}$.*

$r = \frac{7}{36}$ *The product of two negative numbers is positive.*

Solve each equation. Write the solution in simplest form.

1. $y = \frac{4}{5} \div \frac{1}{10}$

2. $15 \div \frac{5}{8} = k$

3. $r = -25 \div 1\frac{3}{7}$

4. $5\frac{1}{3} \div \left(-\frac{3}{8}\right) = t$

5. $f = -\frac{15}{16} \div \left(-\frac{3}{4}\right)$

6. $7\frac{1}{2} \div \left(-2\frac{1}{2}\right) = y$

Evaluate each expression.

7. $a \div b$ if $a = -10\frac{5}{6}$ and $b = 4\frac{1}{3}$

8. $r \div (s + t)$ if $r = 10$, $s = -4\frac{3}{8}$, $t = -1\frac{5}{8}$

9. $a^2 \div y$ if $a = -9$ and $y = -\frac{1}{3}$

7-8 Practice

Dividing Fractions

Solve each equation. Write the solution in simplest form.

1. $\frac{3}{4} \div \frac{9}{10} = j$

2. $s = -\frac{2}{3} \div \frac{6}{11}$

3. $p = \frac{10}{13} \div 15$

4. $r = -6 \div \left(-2\frac{1}{3}\right)$

5. $n = 3\frac{1}{2} \div 2\frac{1}{3}$

6. $5\frac{1}{3} \div (-6) = \ell$

7. $a = \frac{2}{3} \div \frac{3}{4}$

8. $f = 18 \div (-3)$

9. $c = \frac{4}{5} \div \frac{3}{10}$

10. $2\frac{1}{2} \div 3\frac{3}{5} = k$

11. $\frac{4}{9} \div (-6) = b$

12. $m = 5\frac{3}{4} \div \frac{2}{3}$

13. $0.12 \div 16 = g$

14. $h = -6.5 \div 8$

15. $-3.5 \div (-2.75) = d$

Evaluate each expression.

16. $c \div d$ if $c = \frac{1}{3}$ and $d = 2\frac{1}{2}$

17. $a \div b^2$ if $a = -\frac{3}{4}$ and $b = \frac{4}{5}$

18. $x^2 \div y$ if $x = \frac{2}{3}$ and $y = -\frac{3}{2}$

19. $m^2 \div y^2$ if $m = 2\frac{1}{2}$ and $y = 5$

20. What is the value of $\frac{18}{4\frac{1}{2}}$?

7-9 Study Guide

Solving Equations

Solve equations containing rational numbers the same way you solve integer equations.

Examples

1 Solve $-\frac{2}{3}m = \frac{10}{21}$.

$$-\frac{3}{2} \times -\frac{2}{3}m = -\frac{3}{2} \times \frac{10}{21}$$

$$m = -\frac{5}{7}$$

Multiply each side by $-\frac{3}{2}$, the multiplicative inverse of $-\frac{2}{3}$.

Check: $-\frac{2}{3} \times \left(-\frac{5}{7}\right) \overset{?}{=} \frac{10}{21}$

$$\frac{10}{21} = \frac{10}{21} \checkmark$$

2 Solve $-\frac{3}{8} = \frac{t}{5}$.

$$5 \times \left(-\frac{3}{8}\right) = 5 \times \frac{t}{5}$$

Multiply each side by 5.

$$-\frac{15}{8} = t$$

$$-1\frac{7}{8} = t$$

Check: $-\frac{3}{8} \overset{?}{=} -\frac{15}{8} \div 5$

$$-\frac{3}{8} \overset{?}{=} -\frac{15}{8} \times \frac{1}{5}$$

$$-\frac{3}{8} = -\frac{3}{8} \checkmark$$

Solve each equation. Check your solution.

1. $3m = -84$

2. $\frac{y}{5} = -9$

3. $-\frac{1}{2}p = 4.6$

4. $c \div 0.2 = 12$

5. $\frac{k}{1.2} = -5.5$

6. $y - \frac{3}{5} = -6$

7. $\frac{v}{8} = -3.2$

8. $\frac{t}{1.5} = -8$

9. $4.9 = \frac{x}{0.3}$

10. $3\frac{1}{2}n = 7\frac{7}{8}$

11. $-\frac{2}{3} = 8k$

12. $\frac{7}{9}f = 9\frac{1}{3}$

7-9 Practice

Solving Equations

Solve each equation. Check your solution.

1. $2.3w = 6.9$

2. $-\frac{1}{3}y + \frac{2}{9} = \frac{1}{2}$

3. $4.2 = \frac{c}{0.7}$

4. $\frac{3}{5}a - (-4) = 5$

5. $3\frac{1}{2}m = 6\frac{2}{3}$

6. $-\frac{t}{4} = -\frac{7}{8}$

7. $\frac{b}{2.6} = -3.8$

8. $-2.4y - 6.3 = -18.3$

9. $7x = -23$

10. $\frac{x}{6.3} = 63$

11. $b - (-0.07) = 4.5$

12. $-\frac{2}{3}c = 8.7$

13. $\frac{m}{-\frac{2}{3}} = \frac{3}{10}$

14. $-\frac{2}{7}k = \frac{3}{10}$

15. $\frac{2}{3}x - \frac{1}{5} = -2\frac{3}{10}$

16. $6.4s + 3.3 = 12.5$

17. $1\frac{1}{2}t = 3\frac{2}{3}$

18. $-\frac{7}{8}p + 1\frac{1}{4} = 18$

© Glencoe/McGraw-Hill

58

Mathematics: Applications and Connections, Course 3

7-10 Study Guide

Solving Inequalities

You can solve inequalities that involve rational numbers by using the same steps you used to solve inequalities with integers.

Example   Solve $5 + \frac{1}{3}y < 2\frac{1}{2}$.

$$5 + \frac{1}{3}y < 2\frac{1}{2}$$
$$5 + \frac{1}{3}y - 5 < 2\frac{1}{2} - 5$$
$$\frac{1}{3}y < -2\frac{1}{2}$$
$$3\left(\frac{1}{3}y\right) < 3\left(-2\frac{1}{2}\right)$$
$$y < -7\frac{1}{2}$$

The numbers less than $-7\frac{1}{2}$ make up the solution set. The number line below shows the solution.

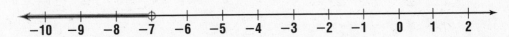

Solve each inequality. Graph the solution on a number line.

1. $a + 2\frac{1}{3} < -\frac{1}{6}$
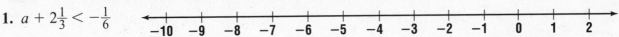

2. $1\frac{1}{8} - b \geq \frac{7}{16}$
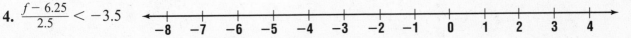

3. $-0.4c \leq 0.9$
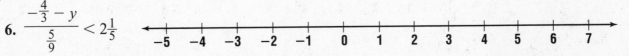

4. $\frac{f - 6.25}{2.5} < -3.5$
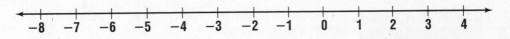

5. $\frac{3}{2}d - 4 \geq \frac{7}{8}$
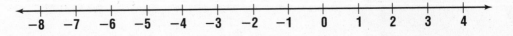

6. $\frac{-\frac{4}{3} - y}{\frac{5}{9}} < 2\frac{1}{5}$
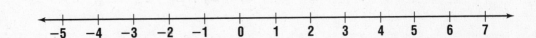
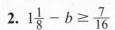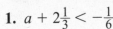

© Glencoe/McGraw-Hill

59

Mathematics: Applications and Connections, Course 3

7-10 Practice

Solving Inequalities

Solve each inequality. Show the solution on the number line.

1. $2x + 9 > 25$

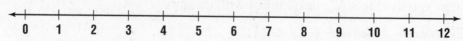

2. $\frac{m}{3} - 7 < 11$

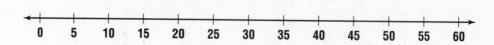

3. $\frac{2x}{9} - 2 \leq -4$

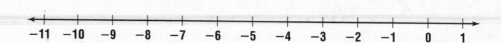

4. $-4.4 > \frac{b}{-5} - 4.8$

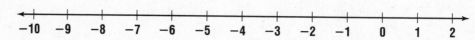

5. $\frac{n - 11}{2} \leq -6$

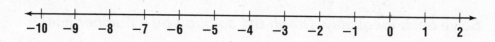

6. $12 - \frac{5z}{4} < 37$

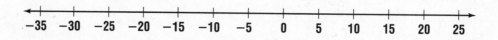

7. $0.47 < \frac{t}{-9} + 0.6$

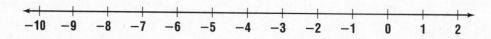

8. $0.3z - 2 \geq 7$

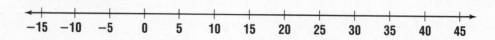

9. $\frac{2}{5}a - 1 > -3$

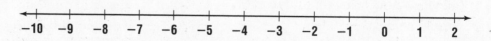

10. $3\frac{1}{4}f \leq 9\frac{2}{7}$

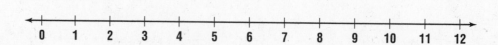

Name_____ Date_____

8-1

Study Guide

Using Proportions

You can use proportions to solve problems.

Example **Of the 360 members of the kennel club who were surveyed, 190 said they would try a new dog food. If the kennel club has 2,100 members, how many could be expected to try the new dog food?**

Let t represent the number of members who might try the new dog food. Write a proportion.

$$\frac{190}{360} = \frac{t}{2,100} \quad \begin{array}{l} \leftarrow \textit{will try new dog food} \\ \leftarrow \textit{kennel club members} \end{array}$$

$190 \cdot 2,100 = 360t \quad \textit{Find the cross products.}$

$399,000 = 360t$

$\frac{399,000}{360} = \frac{360t}{360}$

$1,108 \approx t$

About 1,108 members of the kennel club might be expected to try the new dog food.

Solve.

1. A shop produces 47 surfboards in 6 days. How long will it take them to make 423 surfboards?

2. Six bottles of mineral water cost $2.29. How much will 84 bottles of mineral water cost?

3. A recipe for muffins calls for $1\frac{1}{2}$ cups of bran cereal. The recipe makes 12 muffins. How much bran cereal is needed to make 96 muffins?

4. Five out of every 8 people surveyed in Carson City approved of a new golf course. If there are 26,000 people in Carson City, about how many can be expected to approve of the golf course?

5. Ryan's heart beats 216 times in 3 minutes. How many times will it beat in an hour?

6. A sample of fish from a river showed that $\frac{2}{5}$ of the fish were less than one year old. If there are an estimated 8,000 fish in the river, about how many of them are less than one year old?

7. Maria drove her car 250 miles on 10 gallons of gasoline. About how many gallons of gasoline will she need for a 1,250-mile trip?

Practice

Using Proportions

Write a proportion to solve each problem. Then solve.

1. If 18 plums weigh 54 ounces, then 27 plums weigh x ounces.

2. If 40 nails hold 5 rafters, then 96 nails hold r rafters.

3. If 32 addresses are on 2 pages of the address book, then a addresses are on 9 pages.

4. If 2 quarts fill 8 cups, then 5 quarts fill c cups.

5. If 360 inches of tape are on 3 spools, then t inches of tape are on 10 spools.

6. If 81 rivets are on 3 panels, then r rivets are on 13 panels.

7. If 60 sliced mushrooms are on 4 pizzas, then m sliced mushrooms are on 15 pizzas.

8. If 8 carpets form a 5-inch-high pile, then c carpets form a 30-inch-high pile.

9. If Crystal assembles 3 clipboards in 2 minutes, then she can assemble c clipboards in 15 minutes.

10. If a heart beats 98 times per minute, then it beats y times per hour.

11. If 1.5 ounces of oil are added to 1 gallon of gasoline, then 9 ounces of oil are added to g gallons of gasoline.

12. Dary can type 3 pages in 18 minutes. How many pages can Dary type in 33 minutes?

8-2 Study Guide

The Percent Proportion

You can use a proportion to find the percent for a fraction.

Example 1   Express $\frac{13}{8}$ as a percent.

$$\frac{13}{8} = \frac{x}{100}$$
$$1{,}300 = 8x$$
$$162.5 = x$$
$$\frac{13}{8} = 162.5\%$$

You can use the percent proportion to solve problems.

$$\frac{P}{B} = \frac{r}{100} \text{ or } \frac{\text{Percentage}}{\text{Base}} = \frac{\text{rate}}{100}$$

Examples   **2**   37.2 is what percent of 186?   **3**   What number is 15% of 280?

$$\frac{P}{B} = \frac{r}{100} \qquad\qquad\qquad \frac{P}{B} = \frac{r}{100}$$

$$\frac{37.2}{186} = \frac{r}{100} \qquad\qquad\qquad \frac{P}{280} = \frac{15}{100}$$

$$3{,}720 = 186r \qquad\qquad\qquad 100P = 4{,}200$$
$$20 = r \qquad\qquad\qquad\qquad\quad P = 42$$

37.2 is 20% of 186.   42 is 15% of 280.

Express each fraction as a percent.

1. $\frac{23}{100}$ 2. $\frac{3}{4}$ 3. $\frac{11}{20}$ 4. $\frac{13}{25}$ 5. $\frac{29}{50}$

6. $\frac{7}{8}$ 7. $\frac{7}{16}$ 8. $\frac{7}{25}$ 9. $\frac{2}{5}$ 10. $\frac{13}{40}$

Write a percent proportion to solve each problem. Then solve. Round to the nearest tenth.

11. What is 40% of 160?   12. 75 is what percent of 375?

13. 45 is 25% of what number?   14. 14.5 is 5% of what number?

15. Find 12% of 260.   16. 63 is what percent of 420?

8-2 Practice

The Percent Proportion

Express each fraction as a percent.

1. $\frac{17}{100}$

2. $\frac{16}{25}$

3. $\frac{3}{4}$

4. $\frac{7}{8}$

5. $\frac{31}{1,000}$

6. $\frac{5}{5}$

7. $\frac{12}{16}$

8. $\frac{7}{10}$

9. $\frac{17}{20}$

10. $\frac{4}{9}$

11. $\frac{1}{3}$

12. $\frac{5}{6}$

Match each question with its corresponding proportion.

13. What number is 12% of 6?

    a. $\frac{6}{12} = \frac{x}{100}$

14. 6 is what percent of 12?

    b. $\frac{x}{6} = \frac{12}{100}$

15. 6 is 12% of what number?

    c. $\frac{6}{x} = \frac{12}{100}$

Write a percent proportion to solve each problem. Then solve. Round to the nearest tenth.

16. Find 62.5% of 32.

17. What is 19% of 200?

18. 6 is what percent of 72?

19. 16 is 40% of what number?

20. 22 is what percent of 70?

21. 9 is 2% of what number?

22. What is 35% of 84?

23. 42 is what percent of 150?

24. Kleema owns 40 music CD's. Fifteen of her CD's are recordings done by rap groups. What percent of her CD collection is rap music?

8-3 Study Guide

Integration: Algebra
The Percent Equation

To solve percent problems, you can use the equation $P = RB$, where
P = percentage, R = rate, and B = base.

Examples

1 What number is 16% of 245?   *Estimate: $16\% \approx \frac{1}{5}$; $\frac{1}{5} \times 250 = 50$.*

$P = RB$
$P = 0.16(245)$ *Replace R with 16% or 0.16 and B with 245.*
$P = 39.2$

39.2 is 16% of 245.   *Compare to the estimate.*

2 45 is 15% of what number?   *Estimate: $15\% \approx \frac{1}{5}$; 45 is $\frac{1}{5}$ of 225.*

$P = RB$
$45 = 0.15B$ *Replace P with 45 and R with 15% or 0.15.*
$45 \div 0.15 = 0.15B \div 0.15$ *Divide each side by 0.15.*
$300 = B$

45 is 15% of 300.   *Compare to the estimate.*

3 What percent of 750 is 60?

$P = RB$
$60 = R(750)$
$60 \div 750 = R(750) \div 750$ *Replace P with 60 and B with 750.*
$0.08 = R$ *Divide each side by 750.*

8% of 750 is 60.

Solve.

1. What percent of 80 is 12?

2. What is 18% of 110?

3. Find 2% of 1,600.

4. 75 is 20% of what number?

5. What percent of 42 is 63?

6. What is 5.5% of 90?

7. 64% of what number is 288?

8. Find 88% of $17.50.

9. What is 115% of 90?

10. $5 is what percent of $70?

8-3 Practice

Integration: Algebra
The Percent Equation

Write an equation in the form RB= P for each problem. Then solve.

1. What number is 32% of 200?

2. What percent of 60 is 12?

3. 16 is 40% of what number?

4. Find $12\frac{1}{2}$% of 72.

5. 30% of what amount is $2,400?

6. $15 is what percent of $240?

7. What percent of 120 is 48?

8. 6 is what percent of 200?

Solve.

9. Find 106% of 55.

10. What percent of 80 is 15?

11. $4 is what percent of $50?

12. Find 0.5% of 640.

13. 35% of what number is 56?

14. What percent of 1,000 is 2?

15. What is 2.3% of 610?

16. 96 is 75% of what number?

17. 91 is 140% of what number?

18. What percent of 200 is 400?

19. How much sales tax, at a rate of 5.5%, is due on the sale of a $8,696 car?

20. A surprise quiz was passed by 24 out of 28 students. What percent passed?

8-4 Study Guide

Large and Small Percents

To express a percent greater than 100% or less than 1% as a fraction, write the percent as a fraction with a denominator of 100 and simplify.

Examples

1 $0.4\% = \frac{0.4}{100}$

$= \frac{4}{1,000}$

$= \frac{1}{250}$

2 $175\% = \frac{175}{100}$

$= 1\frac{75}{100}$

$= 1\frac{3}{4}$

3 $\frac{1}{6}\% = \frac{\frac{1}{6}}{100}$

$= \frac{1}{6} \div 100$

$= \frac{1}{6} \times \frac{1}{100}$

$= \frac{1}{600}$

To express a percent greater than 100% or less than 1% as a decimal, write the percent as a fraction with a denominator of 100 and then express the fraction as a decimal.

Examples

4 $254\% = \frac{254}{100}$

$= 2.54$

5 $0.05\% = \frac{0.05}{100}$

$= \frac{5}{10,000}$

$= 0.0005$

6 $\frac{5}{8}\% = \frac{\frac{5}{8}}{100}$

$= \frac{5}{8} \div 100$

$= \frac{5}{8} \times \frac{1}{100}$

$= \frac{5}{800}$

$= 0.00625$

Express each percent as a fraction or mixed number in simplest form.

1. 0.8%

2. 0.09%

3. 853%

4. 420.5%

5. 674%

6. $\frac{1}{2}$%

7. $\frac{3}{50}$%

8. 0.15%

Express each percent as a decimal.

9. 716%

10. 0.07%

11. 1,463%

12. 0.9%

13. $\frac{3}{10}$%

14. 0.004%

15. 900%

16. $\frac{3}{5}$%

8-4 Practice

Large and Small Percents

Express each percent as a fraction or mixed number in simplest form.

1. 0.15%

2. 250%

3. 0.06%

4. 0.5%

5. 165%

6. 350%

7. 0.25%

8. 0.1%

9. 110%

10. $62\frac{1}{2}$%

11. $\frac{3}{4}$%

12. 150%

Express each percent as a decimal.

13. 316%

14. 0.02%

15. 0.15%

16. 2,345%

17. $\frac{1}{4}$%

18. $\frac{1}{2}$%

19. Order $\frac{1}{2}$%, 50%, 5%, and 500% from least to greatest.

20. Write 1.07%, 0.7%, 107%, 0.07%, and 1 in order from greatest to least.

21. Which of the following numbers is the greatest? the least?

   0.9, $\frac{9}{10}$%, 85%, $\frac{1}{2}$

Mathematics: Applications and Connections, Course 3

8-5 **Study Guide**

Percent of Change

To find the percent of increase or decrease, first find the amount of the increase or decrease. Then find the ratio of that amount to the original amount and express it as a percent.

Example 1 **Two years ago a bicycle shop sold 675 bicycles. This year, 865 bicycles were sold. To the nearest percent, what is the percent of increase?**

First, find the amount of change: $865 - 675 = 190$.
Then, find the percent using 675 as the base.

$$\frac{190}{675} = \frac{r}{100}$$

$190 \cdot 100 = 675 \cdot r$
$19{,}000 = 675r$
$28 \approx r$ The percent of change is 28%.

A percent of discount is a percent of decrease.

Example 2 **A VCR that usually sells for $365 is on sale for 20% off. What is the sale price?**

Method 1

First, find the amount of the discount.
    $RB = P$
$0.20 \cdot 365 = P$
    $73 = P$
Then, subtract the discount from the regular price.
    $365 - 73 = 292$

The sale price is $292.

Method 2

First, find the percent paid.
$100\% - 20\% = 80\%$
Then, find the sale price.
    $RB \quad = P$
$0.80 \cdot 365 = P$
    $292 = P$

Find each percent of change. Round to the nearest percent.

1. original: $10
    new: $8

2. original: 85
    new: 112

3. original: 120
    new: 200

4. original: $75
    new: $30

Find the sale price of each item to the nearest cent.

5. $465 golf clubs, 20% off

6. $129 telephone, 30% off

7. $17.99 video, 40% off

8. $395 guitar, 10% off

Mathematics: Applications and Connections, Course 3

8-5 Practice

Percent of Change

Find each percent of change. Round to the nearest percent.

1. original: $4
   new: $4.44

2. original: $25
   new: $30

3. original: $400
   new: $380

4. original: $65
   new: $50

5. original: $140
   new: $100

6. original: $20
   new: $12

Find the sale price of each item to the nearest cent.

7. $55 sport bag, 20% off

8. $8.99 bag of tube socks, 30% off

9. $89.99 portable radio, 10% off

10. $54.99 toaster oven, 27% off

11. $42 jumper set, 25% off

12. $189 pendant, 30% off

Find the selling price for each item given the amount paid by the store and the markup. Round to the nearest cent.

13. $240 grill, 25% markup

14. $580 refrigerator, 30% markup

15. $160 microwave, 20% markup

16. $150 chair, 35% markup

17. $59.99 running shoes, 15% markup

18. $99.99 watch, 20% markup

19. Find the percent of change in price if the old selling price was $20 and the new selling price is $15.

20. Find the percent of change in price if the old selling price was $13 and the new selling price is $15.

8-6 Study Guide

Simple Interest

To find simple interest, use the formula $I = prt$. Interest (I) is the charge for the use of money. Principal (p) is the amount of money. Rate (r) is a percent of annual interest. Time (t) is the time in years that the money is used.

Examples   **1**   **Find the interest earned on $490 deposited in a savings account at $8\frac{1}{2}\%$ per year for 6 months.**

$I = prt$ $p = \$490$, $r = 8\frac{1}{2}\%$, or 0.085,
$I = 490(0.085)\left(\frac{6}{12}\right)$ $t = 6$ out of 12 months or $\frac{6}{12}$

$I = 20.825$ or $\$20.83$

Find the total amount of money in the savings account.

$\$490.00 + \$20.83 = \$510.83$ *Add the interest to the original amount.*

2   **Find the annual rate of simple interest if $3,600 was borrowed and $4,248 was repaid 18 months later.**

The amount of interest was $\$4,248 - \$3,600$ or $\$648$.

$I = prt$
$648 = 3,600(r)\left(\frac{18}{12}\right)$ $I = \$648$, $p = \$3,600$, $t = \frac{18}{12}$
$648 = 5,400r$
$0.12 = r$ The interest rate was 0.12 or 12%.

Find the simple interest to the nearest cent.

1. $500 at 7% for 4 years

2. $2,800 at 6.5% for 18 months

3. $1,050 at 18% for 3 months

4. $725 at 5.5% for 2 years

Find the total amount in each account to the nearest cent.

5. $1,250 at 5% for 1 year

6. $600 at 14.5% for 9 months

7. $276 at 8% for 3 years

8. $4,500 at 9% for 6 months

Find the annual rate of simple interest.

9. principal: $1,700; total amount after 3 years: $2,210

10. principal: $6,300; total amount after 6 months: $6,772.50

Name_____ Date_____

8-6 Practice

Simple Interest

Find the simple interest to the nearest cent.

1. $250 at 20% for 1 year

2. $300 at 15% for 14 months

3. $75 at 6.5% for 9 months

4. $625 at 18.5% for 1 year

5. $3,284 at 15.5% for 2 years

6. $6,850 at 16% for 30 months

7. $170 at 3% for 4 years

8. $2,341 at 16.2% for 6 months

Find the total amount in each account to the nearest cent.

9. $300 at 6% for 3 years

10. $275 at 5.5% for 20 months

11. $1,000 at 5.5% for 9 months

12. $16 at 3% for 6 years

13. $298 at 4.5% for 3 months

14. $7,184 at 5.25% for 10 months

15. Suppose $5,000 is placed in a savings account for 3 years. Find the simple interest if the interest rate is 5%.

16. A savings account starts with $725. If the simple interest rate is 7%, find the total amount in the account after 18 months.

17. A savings account starts with $250. It earns $30 in 2 years. Find the rate of interest.

65

8-7 Study Guide

Integration: Geometry
Similar Polygons

A **polygon** is a closed figure in a plane and is formed by three or more line segments that meet only at their endpoints.

Two polygons are **similar** if their corresponding angles are congruent and their corresponding sides are in proportion.

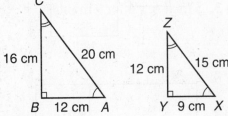

Example 1 $\angle A \cong \angle X$ $\frac{XY}{AB} = \frac{9}{12} = \frac{3}{4}$

$\angle B \cong \angle Y$ $\frac{YZ}{BC} = \frac{12}{16} = \frac{3}{4}$

$\angle C \cong \angle Z$ $\frac{XZ}{AC} = \frac{15}{20} = \frac{3}{4}$

The corresponding angles are equal.
The corresponding sides are in proportion.
$\triangle ABC \sim \triangle XYZ$ The symbol ~ means "is similar to."

You can use proportions to solve problems involving similar figures.

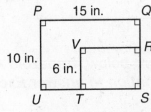

Example 2   **The two quadrilaterals are similar.**
Find the length of side $\overline{VR}$.

$\overline{PU}$ corresponds to $\overline{VT}$.
$\overline{PQ}$ corresponds to $\overline{VR}$.

Write a proportion.   Substitute values.   Find cross products.

$\frac{PU}{VT} = \frac{PQ}{VR}$ $\frac{10}{6} = \frac{15}{x}$ $10x = 90$
                                                            $x = 9$

The length of $\overline{VR}$ is 9 inches.

Tell whether each pair of polygons is similar.

1.

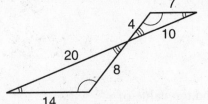

2.

3.

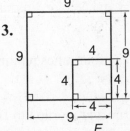

$\triangle ABC \sim \triangle ADE$. Use this information to answer Exercises 4-6.

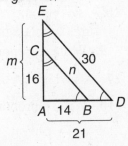

4.   List all pairs of corresponding angles.

5.   Write a proportion and solve for m.

6.   Write a proportion and solve for n.

8-7 Practice

Integration: Geometry
Similar Polygons

Tell whether each pair of polygons are similar.

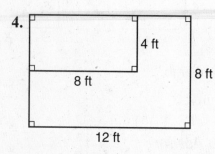

1. 10 ft   8 ft   15 ft   12 ft

2. 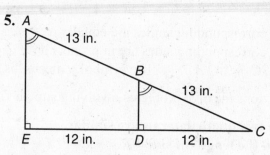 3 cm   3.5 cm   3.5 cm   6 cm   7 cm   7 cm

3. 101 m   100 m   150 m   151 m

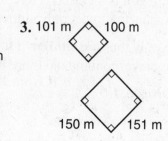

4. 4 ft   8 ft   8 ft   12 ft

5. A   13 in.   B   13 in.   C   E   12 in.   D   12 in.

In the figure below, trapezoid ABCD ~ trapezoid EFGH. Use this information to answer Exercises 6-10.

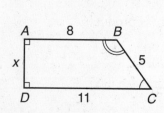

A   8   B   x   5   D   11   C

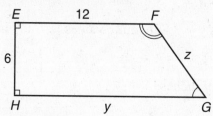

E   12   F   6   z   H   y   G

6. List all pairs of corresponding angles.

7. Write four ratios relating the corresponding sides.

8. Write a proportion to find the missing measure x. Then find the value of x.

9. Write a proportion to find the missing measure y. Then find the value of y.

10. Write a proportion to find the missing measure z. Then find the value of z.

Mathematics: Applications and Connections, Course 3

8-8 Study Guide

Indirect Measurement

You can use a proportion to find a measurement indirectly.

Example   A bridge from Carl's Cave (C) to Bluff Lookout (B)
across a river is 600 feet long. The distance from
Arborville (A) to Bluff Lookout is 900 feet. The distance
from Arborville to Emmeryville (E) is 1,000 feet. How
far is it from Bluff Lookout to Deadman's Rock (D)?

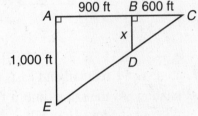

$$\frac{AC}{BC} = \frac{AE}{BD}$$ *Write a proportion.*

$$\frac{900 + 600}{600} = \frac{1,000}{x}$$ *Substitute.*

$$1,500x = 600,000$$ *Find cross products.*

$$x = 400$$

It is 400 feet from Bluff Lookout to Deadman's Rock.

Write a proportion for each problem and then solve it. Assume the triangles are similar.

1. A statue casts a shadow 30 feet long.
   At the same time, a person who is 5
   feet tall casts a shadow that is 6 feet
   long. How tall is the statue?

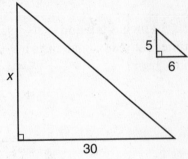

2. A guide wire is attached to the top
   of a radio tower. It attaches to the
   ground 40 feet from its base.
   Angelica is 5 feet tall. When she
   stands so her head touches the
   guide wire, she is 2 feet from the
   point where it attaches to the
   ground. How tall is the tower?

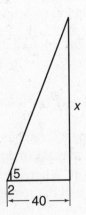

*Mathematics: Applications
and Connections, Course 3*

Practice

Indirect Measurement

Write a proportion for each problem and solve it. Assume the figures are similar.

1. A photograph measuring 8 inches wide and 10 inches long is enlarged to make a wall mural. The mural is 60 inches wide. How long is the mural?

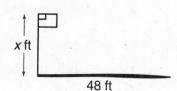

2. Lena is $5\frac{1}{2}$ feet tall and casts an 8-foot shadow. At the same time, a flagpole casts a 48-foot shadow. How tall is the flagpole?

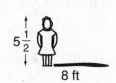

3. Bobbi is 30 inches tall and casts a 12-inch shadow. At the same time, her teddy bear casts a 9-inch shadow. How tall is Bobbi's bear?

4. Bob and Ted carefully place wooden stakes to measure the length of Muddy Pond. How long is Muddy Pond?

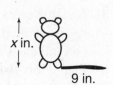

5. Janice is trimming a large piece of parachute fabric to make a store-window display 6-feet high. When she discards the scrap, how long will the remaining piece of fabric be?

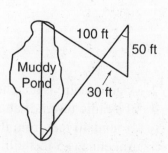

8-9 Study Guide

Scale Drawings and Models

In a **scale drawing,** the lengths on the drawing are proportional to the actual lengths. Maps and blueprints are examples of scale drawings.

Example   **On this map, each one-half centimeter square represents 5 kilometers. Find the distance from Horse Rock to East Bank Lookout.**

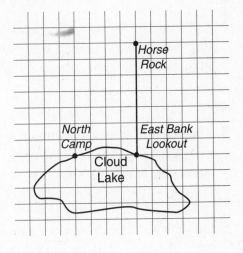

Use the scale to form a proportion. Then solve the proportion.

$$\frac{\frac{1}{2} \text{ cm}}{5 \text{ km}} = \frac{3\frac{1}{2} \text{ cm}}{x \text{ km}}$$

$$\frac{1}{2}x = 5\left(3\frac{1}{2}\right)$$

$$\frac{1}{2}x = 17\frac{1}{2}$$

$$x = 35$$

It is 35 kilometers from Horse Rock to East Bank Lookout.

The figures show scale drawings of two types of kites. In the top drawing, the side of each square represents 2 inches. In the bottom drawing, the side of each square represents 3 inches. Find the actual length of each segment.

1. $\overline{AB}$

2. $\overline{CD}$

3. $\overline{CE}$

4. $\overline{ED}$

5. $\overline{QT}$

6. $\overline{QS}$

7. $\overline{RU}$

8. $\overline{UT}$

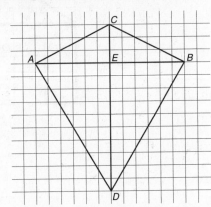

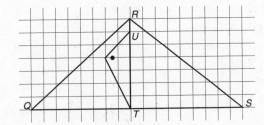

8-9 Practice

Scale Drawings and Models

The distance on a map is given. Find the actual distance, if the scale on the map is 1 in. = 60 miles.

1. 2 in.   **2.** $3\frac{1}{2}$ in.   **3.** $2\frac{3}{4}$ in.   **4.** $5\frac{1}{4}$ in.

Solve.

5. Abe prepares a scale drawing of an office building. Abe uses a scale of 1 in. = 12 feet. The drawing of the building is $9\frac{1}{2}$ inches high. How high is the building?

6. Lin draws a scale drawing of a miniature computer diode. She uses a scale of 1 in. = 0.01 in. Lin's drawing is 7.5 inches wide. How wide is the computer diode?

The figure at the right is a scale drawing of a playhouse. In the drawing, the side of each square represents 2 feet. Find actual length of each segment.

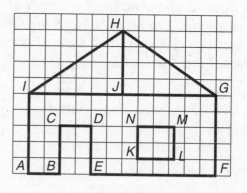

7. the width of the house, *IG*

8. the height of the wall, *FG*

9. the width of the door, *BE*

10. the height of the roof, *HJ*

11. the height of the window, *KN*

12. the length of the window, *KL*

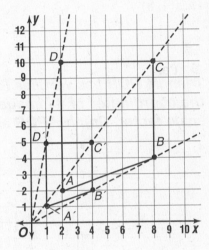

8-10 Study Guide

Integration: Geometry
Dilations

Enlarging or reducing a figure is called a **dilation**. A dilated figure is similar to the original figure. The ratio of the new figure to the original is called the scale factor.

Example   **Graph trapezoid *ABCD* with vertices**
$A(2, 2)$, $B(8, 4)$, $C(8, 10)$, $D(2, 10)$. Graph
its dilation with a scale factor of 0.5.

To find the vertices of the dilation image, multiply each coordinate in the ordered pairs by 0.5.
$A(2, 2) \rightarrow (2 \cdot 0.5, 2 \cdot 0.5) \rightarrow A'(1, 1)$
$B(8, 4) \rightarrow (8 \cdot 0.5, 4 \cdot 0.5) \rightarrow B'(4, 2)$
$C(8, 10) \rightarrow (8 \cdot 0.5, 10 \cdot 0.5) \rightarrow C'(4, 5)$
$D(2, 10) \rightarrow (2 \cdot 0.5, 10 \cdot 0.5) \rightarrow D'(1, 5)$

Graph trapezoid $A'B'C'D'$.

To check the graph, draw lines from the origin though each of the vertices of the original figure. The vertices of the dilated figure should lie on the same lines.

Triangle LMN has vertices
L(8, 2), M(10, 8), N(4, 6). Find
the coordinates of its image
for a dilation with each given
scale factor. Graph △LMN
and each dilation.

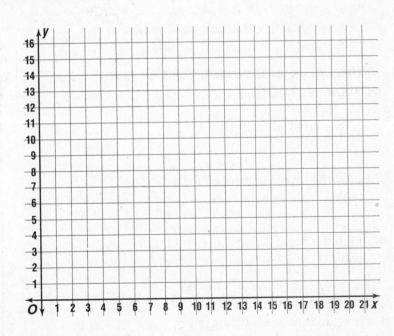

1. 0.5

2. 1.5

3. 2

Practice

Integration: Geometry
Dilations

Find the coordinates of the image of each point for a dilation with a scale factor of $\frac{3}{2}$.

1. $A(4, 8)$

2. $B(3, 10)$

3. $C(-2, -5)$

Triangle PQR has vertices P(−2, 2), Q(3, 2), and R(0, −2). Find the coordinates of its image for a dilation with each given scale factor. Graph △PQR and each dilation.

4. 2

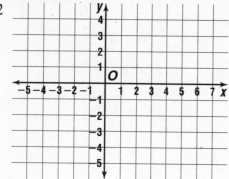

5. $\frac{1}{2}$

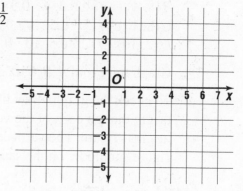

In the figure at the right, △A′OB′ is a dilation of △AOB.

6. Find the image of $A(3, 4)$ for a dilation with a scale factor of 3.

7. Find the image of $B(6, 0)$ for a dilation with a scale factor of 1.3.

8. Find the scale factor if $OA = 12$, $OB = 9$, and $OA' = 72$.

9. Find the length of $A'B'$ if AB is 32 inches long and the scale factor is 1.5.

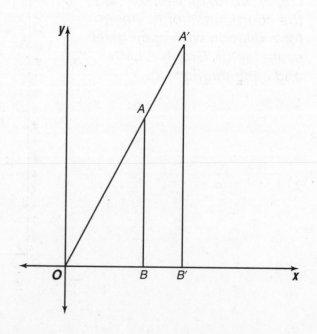

Name _____ **Date** _____

9-1 Study Guide

Square Roots

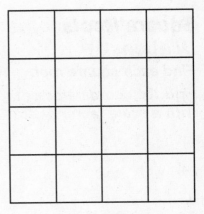

The area of a square is equal to the square of the length of its side. For the square shown, $A = 4^2$ or 16.

The length of a side of a square is equal to the square root of the area. For the square shown, 4 is the square root of 16.

If $x^2 = y$, then x is a **square root** of y. The symbol $\sqrt{\ }$ is called a **radical sign.** Read $\sqrt{16}$ as "the square root of 16."

Examples

x	$x^2 = y$	$\sqrt{y} = x$	
4	$4 \times 4 = 4^2 = 16$	$\sqrt{16} = 4$	*principal square root*
−4	$-4 \times -4 = (-4)^2 = 16$	$-\sqrt{16} = -4$	*negative square root*
1.5	$1.5^2 = 2.25$	$\sqrt{2.25} = 1.5$	
−1.5	$(-1.5)^2 = 2.25$	$-\sqrt{2.25} = -1.5$	

To find a square root, think of a number that when multiplied by itself (squared) equals the number under the radical sign.

Examples   Find each square root.

$\sqrt{\dfrac{49}{64}} \longrightarrow \dfrac{7}{8} \times \dfrac{7}{8} = \dfrac{49}{64} \longrightarrow \sqrt{\dfrac{49}{64}} = \dfrac{7}{8}$

$\sqrt{-0.25} \longrightarrow (-0.5)^2 = 0.25 \longrightarrow -\sqrt{0.25} = -0.5$

Find each square root.

1. $\sqrt{100}$

2. $-\sqrt{144}$

3. $\sqrt{81}$

4. $-\sqrt{0.64}$

5. $\sqrt{\dfrac{9}{16}}$

6. $-\sqrt{6.25}$

7. $\sqrt{169}$

8. $-\sqrt{25}$

9. $-\sqrt{121}$

10. $\sqrt{\dfrac{25}{81}}$

11. $-\sqrt{0.16}$

12. $\sqrt{225}$

13. $-\sqrt{10,000}$

14. $\sqrt{400}$

15. $-\sqrt{1.21}$

16. $\sqrt{1.44}$

© Glencoe/McGraw-Hill

70

Mathematics: Applications and Connections, Course 3

9-1 Practice

Square Roots

Find each square root.

1. $\sqrt{9}$

2. $\sqrt{36}$

3. $\sqrt{25}$

4. $\sqrt{81}$

5. $-\sqrt{144}$

6. $\sqrt{256}$

7. $\sqrt{441}$

8. $\sqrt{324}$

9. $-\sqrt{121}$

10. $-\sqrt{576}$

11. $\sqrt{900}$

12. $-\sqrt{289}$

13. $\sqrt{10.24}$

14. $-\sqrt{\frac{25}{49}}$

15. $\sqrt{2.25}$

16. $\sqrt{\frac{9}{25}}$

17. $-\sqrt{0.25}$

18. $\sqrt{\frac{36}{100}}$

19. Find two square roots of 361. Explain which is *not* the principal square root.

20. If the area of a square is 5.29 square inches, what is the length of the side of the square?

21. If the area of a square is 1 square meter, how many centimeters long is each side?

9-2

Study Guide

Estimating Square Roots

Many numbers are not perfect squares. You can estimate square roots for these numbers.

Examples   **1**   **Estimate $\sqrt{200}$.**

$14^2 = 196$ *196 is a perfect square.*
$15^2 = 225$ *225 is a perfect square.*

$196 < 200 < 225$ *200 is between 196 and 225.*
$14^2 < 200 < 15^2$

$14 < \sqrt{200} < 15$ *The square root of 200 is between 14 and 15.*

Since 200 is closer to 196 than to 225, the best whole number estimate for $\sqrt{200}$ is 14.

2   **Estimate $\sqrt{83.2}$.**

$9^2 = 81$
$10^2 = 100$

$81 < 83.2 < 100$ *83.2 is between 81 and 100.*
$9^2 < 83.2 < 10^2$
$9 < \sqrt{83.2} < 10$

Since 83.2 is closer to 81 than to 100, the best whole number estimate for $\sqrt{83.2}$ is 9.

Estimate to the nearest whole number.

1. $\sqrt{79}$ **2.** $\sqrt{24}$ **3.** $\sqrt{38}$ **4.** $\sqrt{103}$

5. $\sqrt{230}$ **6.** $\sqrt{85}$ **7.** $\sqrt{898}$ **8.** $\sqrt{1610}$

9. $\sqrt{15.5}$ **10.** $\sqrt{34.9}$ **11.** $\sqrt{50.6}$ **12.** $\sqrt{170}$

9-2 Practice

Estimating Square Roots

Estimate to the nearest whole number.

1. $\sqrt{84}$

2. $\sqrt{10}$

3. $\sqrt{69}$

4. $\sqrt{99}$

5. $\sqrt{120}$

6. $\sqrt{78}$

7. $\sqrt{250}$

8. $\sqrt{444}$

9. $\sqrt{51}$

10. $\sqrt{178}$

11. $\sqrt{300}$

12. $\sqrt{123}$

13. $\sqrt{199}$

14. $\sqrt{171}$

15. $\sqrt{286}$

16. $\sqrt{730}$

17. $\sqrt{17.8}$

18. $\sqrt{630}$

19. $\sqrt{1,230}$

20. $\sqrt{8.42}$

21. $\sqrt{0.09}$

22. $\sqrt{80.95}$

23. $\sqrt{1.05}$

24. $\sqrt{47.25}$

9-3

Study Guide

The Real Number System

Numbers may be classified into the following sets.

Natural Numbers $\{1, 2, 3, 4, \ldots\}$
Whole Numbers $\{0, 1, 2, 3, 4, \ldots\}$
Integers $\{\ldots, -2, -1, 0, 1, 2, \ldots\}$
Rational Numbers {numbers that can be expressed in the form $\frac{a}{b}$, where a and b are integers and $b \neq 0$}
Irrational Numbers {numbers that cannot be expressed in the form $\frac{a}{b}$, where a and b are integers and $b \neq 0$}
Real Numbers {rational numbers and irrational numbers}

Examples Classify each real number.

1 **0** whole number, integer, rational number

2 **0.777 . . .** Terminating or repeating decimals are rational numbers, since they can be expressed as fractions.
$0.777\ldots = \frac{7}{9}$

3 **$\sqrt{0.16}$** Square roots of perfect squares are rational numbers.
$\sqrt{0.16} = 0.4$, a rational number.

4 **$\sqrt{19}$** Square roots of numbers that are not perfect squares may be represented by decimals that do not repeat or terminate. They are irrational numbers.

To solve equations with squares, use your calculator to find square roots.

Examples Solve each equation.

5 $c^2 = 100$
$c = \sqrt{100}$ or $c = -\sqrt{100}$
$c = 10$ or $c = -10$

6 $x^2 = 60$
$x = \sqrt{60}$ or $x = -\sqrt{60}$
60 [2nd] [√] 7.745966692
$x = 7.7$ or $x = -7.7$

Name the set or sets of numbers to which each real number belongs.

1. 23

2. $\frac{7}{8}$

3. $\sqrt{31}$

4. 0.2727272. . .

5. $\frac{5}{11}$

6. 0.12131415. . .

7. $\sqrt{0.81}$

8. -3

Solve each equation. Round solutions to the nearest tenth.

9. $m^2 = 81$

10. $x^2 = 5$

11. $t^2 = 0.49$

12. $n^2 = 1,600$

9-3 Practice

The Real Number System

Name the set or sets of numbers to which each real number belongs.

1. 12

2. $-\sqrt{25}$

3. $\sqrt{13}$

4. $\sqrt{0.36}$

5. $0.373773777\ldots$

6. $0.505050\ldots$

7. $\sqrt{25.0}$

8. $-\sqrt{40}$

9. $\frac{3}{7}$

Find an estimate for each square root. Then graph the square root on the number line.

10. $\sqrt{8}$ 11. $\sqrt{35}$ 12. $\sqrt{71}$ 13. $\sqrt{18}$

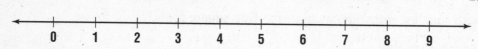

14. $\sqrt{3}$ 15. $-\sqrt{3}$ 16. $\sqrt{5}$ 17. $-\sqrt{7}$

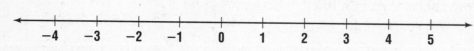

Solve each equation. Round solutions to the nearest tenth.

18. $a^2 = 196$

19. $y^2 = 81$

20. $c^2 = 150$

21. $x^2 = 1.69$

22. $b^2 = 0$

23. $n^2 = 85$

Mathematics: Applications and Connections, Course 3

9-4 Study Guide

The Pythagorean Theorem

The longest side of a right triangle is the **hypotenuse.**
The hypotenuse is the side opposite the right angle.
The other two sides of the triangle are the **legs.**

The **Pythagorean Theorem** relates the lengths of the sides of a right
triangle: For any right triangle, the square of the hypotenuse is equal to the
sum of the squares of the legs. You can use the Pythagorean Theorem to
find the length of a side of a right triangle if the lengths of the other two
sides are known.

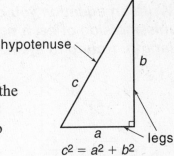

hypotenuse

$c^2 = a^2 + b^2$

legs

Examples   **1** If $a = 30$ and $b = 40$, find c.   **2** If $c = 20$ and $a = 15$, find b.

$c^2 = a^2 + b^2$ $c^2 = a^2 + b^2$
$c^2 = 30^2 + 40^2$ $20^2 = 15^2 + b^2$
$c^2 = 900 + 1,600$ $400 = 225 + b^2$
$c^2 = 2,500$ $400 - 225 = b^2$
$c = \sqrt{2,500}$ $175 = b^2$
$c = 50$ $\sqrt{175} = b$
The length of the hypotenuse is $13.228757 = b$
50 units.   The length of the leg is 13.2 units.

The converse of the Pythagorean Theorem can be used to test whether a
triangle is a right triangle: If the sides of a triangle have lengths a, b, and c
units such that $c^2 = a^2 + b^2$, then the triangle is a right triangle.

Find the missing measure for each right triangle. Round decimal answers to the nearest tenth.

1. $a = 8$ m; $c = 10$ m   **2.** $a = 5$ ft, $b = 12$ ft   **3.** $b = 15$ cm, $c = 25$ cm

4. $a = 7$ km, $c = 12$ km   **5.** $a = 8$ yd, $b = 11$ yd   **6.** $b = 14$ in., $c = 20$ in.

Determine whether each triangle with sides of given lengths is a right triangle.

7. 20, 21, 29   **8.** 7, 24, 25   **9.** 9, 11, 14

9-4 Practice

The Pythagorean Theorem

Write an equation you could use to find the length of the missing side of each right triangle. Then find the missing length. Round to the nearest tenth.

1.
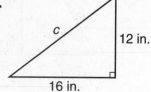
c
12 in.
16 in.

2.
8 cm
c
15 cm

3.
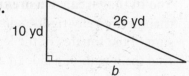
10 yd
26 yd
b

4.
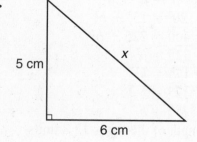
5 cm
x
6 cm

5.
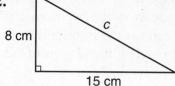
x
12 in.
12 in.

6.
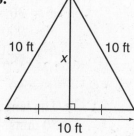
10 ft
x
10 ft
10 ft

7. *a*, 24 ft; *b*, 32 ft

8. *a*, 9 ft; *c*; 16 ft

9. *b*, 5 in.; *c*, 11 in.

10. *a*, 8 cm; *b*, 12 cm

11. *b*, 15 yd; *c*, 21 yd

12. *a*, 6.3 cm; *c*, 12.4 cm

Determine whether each triangle with sides of given lengths is a right triangle.

13. 6 cm, 8 cm, 10 cm

14. 9 mm, 12 mm, 16 mm

15. 18 ft, 80 ft, 82 ft

16. 10 mi, 24 mi, 25 mi

17. 15 cm, 36 cm, 39 cm

18. 16 yd, 30 yd, 34 yd

9-5 Study Guide

Using the Pythagorean Theorem

You can use the Pythagorean Theorem to help you solve problems.

Example   **An ice hockey rink is 200 feet long and 85 feet wide. What is the length of the diagonal of the rink?**

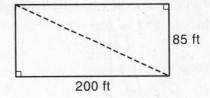
85 ft

200 ft

$c^2 = a^2 + b^2$
$c^2 = 200^2 + 85^2$
$c^2 = 40,000 + 7,225$
$c^2 = 47,225$
$c = \sqrt{47,225}$
$c \approx 217.3$

The length of the diagonal of an ice hockey rink is about 217.3 feet.

The chart shows some Pythagorean triples, numbers that satisfy the Pythagorean Theorem. You can find other Pythagorean triples by finding multiples of these triples.

a	b	c
3	4	5
5	12	13
8	15	17
9	40	41

	a	b	c
original	5	12	13
× 2	10	24	26
× 3	15	36	39
× 4	20	48	52

10-24-26, 15-36-39, and 20-48-52 are members of the 5-12-13 family.

Solve. Round answers to the nearest tenth.

1.
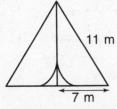
11 m

7 m

What is the height of the center pole?

2.
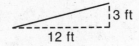
3 ft
12 ft

What is the length of the ramp?

3.
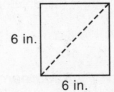
6 in.

6 in.

What is the length of the diagonal?

Mathematics: Applications and Connections, Course 3

9-5 Practice

Using the Pythagorean Theorem

**Write an equation that can be used to answer each question.
Then solve. Round to the nearest tenth.**

1.

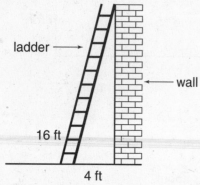

ladder →

← wall

16 ft

4 ft

How high will the ladder reach?

2.

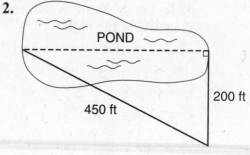

POND

450 ft

200 ft

How far is it across the pond?

3.

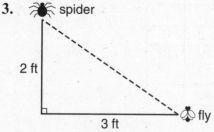

spider

2 ft

3 ft

fly

How far apart are the spider and fly?

4.

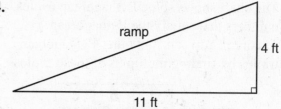

ramp

4 ft

11 ft

How long is the ramp?

5.

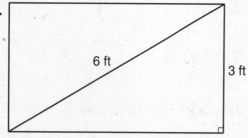

6 ft

3 ft

How long is the tabletop?

6.

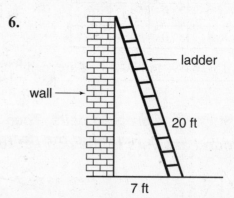

wall →

ladder

20 ft

7 ft

How high will the ladder reach?

**For each Pythagorean triple, find two triples in the
same family.**

7. 7 − 24 − 25

8. 3 − 4 − 5

9. 5 − 12 − 13

9-6

Study Guide

Integration: Geometry
Distance on the Coordinate Plane

You can use the Pythagorean Theorem to find the distance between two points on the coordinate plane.

Example   **Find the distance between the points at (2, −3) and (5, 4).**

Graph the points and connect them with a line segment. Draw a horizontal line through (2, −3) and a vertical line through (5, 4). The lines intersect at (5, −3).

Count units to find the length of each leg of the triangle. Then use the Pythagorean Theorem to find the hypotenuse.

$$c^2 = a^2 + b^2$$
$$c^2 = 3^2 + 7^2$$
$$c^2 = 9 + 49$$
$$c^2 = 58$$
$$c = \sqrt{58}$$
$$c \approx 7.6$$

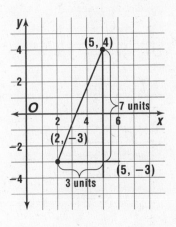

The distance between (2, −3) and (5, 4) is about 7.6 units.

Find the distance between each pair of points whose coordinates are given. Round to the nearest tenth.

1.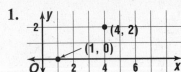

2.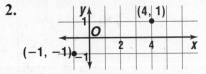

3.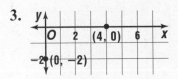

Graph each pair of ordered pairs. Then find the distance between the points. Round to the nearest tenth.

4. (4, 5); (0, 2)

5. (0, −4); (−3, 0)

6. (3, 1); (1, −4)

7. (−1, 1); (−4, 4)

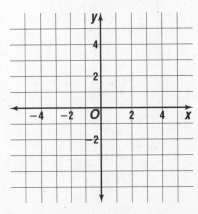

Mathematics: Applications and Connections, Course 3

9-6 Practice

Integration: Geometry
Distance on the Coordinate Plane

Find the distance between each pair of points whose coordinates are given. Round to the nearest tenth.

1.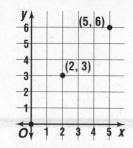

2.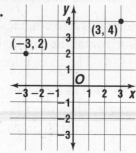

3.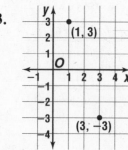

4.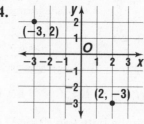

Graph each pair of ordered pairs. Then find the distance between the points. Round to the nearest tenth.

5. $(5, 4)$; $(5, -3)$

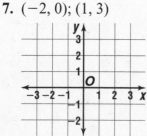

6. $(1, 2)$; $(2, 4)$

7. $(-2, 0)$; $(1, 3)$

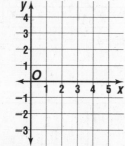

8. $(-2, -3)$; $(3, -4)$

Mathematics: Applications and Connections, Course 3

Name _____ Date _____

9-7 Study Guide

Integration: Geometry
Special Right Triangles

In a 30°-60° right triangle, the length of the side opposite the 30° angle is one-half the length of the hypotenuse. You can use this relationship to solve problems.

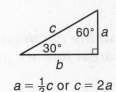

$a = \frac{1}{2}c$ or $c = 2a$

Example 1 **Find the lengths b and c.**

Find c.
$c = 2a$
$c = 2(25)$
$c = 50$

Find b.
$c^2 = a^2 + b^2$
$50^2 = 25^2 + b^2$
$2{,}500 = 625 + b^2$
$2{,}500 - 625 = b^2$
$1{,}875 = b^2$
$\sqrt{1{,}875} = b$
$43.3 \approx b$

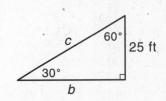

The length of hypotenuse c is 50 feet.
The length of side b is about 43.3 feet.

In a 45°-45° right triangle, the lengths of the legs are equal. You can use this relationship to solve problems.

Example 2 **Find the lengths of a and c.**

Find a.
$a = b$
$a = 15$

Find c.
$c^2 = a^2 + b^2$
$c^2 = 15^2 + 15^2$
$c^2 = 225 + 225$
$c^2 = 450$
$c = \sqrt{450}$
$c \approx 21.2$

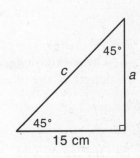

The length of side a is 15 cm.
The length of hypotenuse c is about 21.2 cm.

Find the missing lengths. Round decimal answers to the nearest tenth.

1.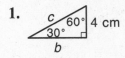

2.

3.

4.

5.

6.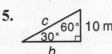

Mathematics: Applications and Connections, Course 3

Name _____ **Date** _____

Practice

Integration: Geometry
Special Right Triangles

Find the missing lengths. Round decimal answers to the nearest tenth.

1.
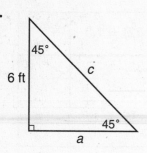

2.
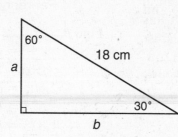

3.
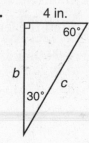

4.
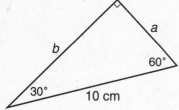

5.
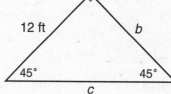

6.
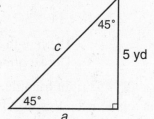

7. The shorter leg of a 30° -60° right triangle is 18 feet. What is the length of the other leg?

8. One leg of a 45° -45° right triangle is 18 inches. Find the length of the hypotenuse.

9. The length of the hypotenuse of a 30° -60° right triangle is 8.5 cm. Find the length of the side opposite the 30° angle.

10. One leg of a 45° -45° right triangle is 33.5 inches. Find the length of the hypotenuse.

10-1 Study Guide

Functions

A **function** connects a number, n, to another number, $f(n)$, by a rule. Read $f(n)$ as "the function of n." The set of input values, values of n, is called the **domain.** The set of output values, values of $f(n)$, is called the **range.**

Example   A temperature given in degrees Fahrenheit has a corresponding Celsius temperature. Find the corresponding temperature for {0°, 32°, 65°, 98.6°} if $f(n) = (n - 32) \div 1.8$.

Fahrenheit n	$(n - 32) \div 1.8$	Celsius $f(n)$
0	$(0 - 32) \div 1.8$	−17.8
32	$(32 - 32) \div 1.8$	0
65	$(65 - 32) \div 1.8$	18.3
98.6	$(98.6 - 32) \div 1.8$	37

Let n equal degrees Fahrenheit. The domain is {0, 32, 65, 98.6}. Use the rule $(n - 32) \div 1.8$. Substitute as shown in the function table. The range is {−17.8, 0, 18.3, 37}.

Complete each function table.

1.

n	$n - 10$	$f(n)$
−10		
0		
15		
20		
32		

2.

n	$2n$	$f(n)$
−3		
0		
2		
5		

3.

n	$3n + 1$	$f(n)$
2		
10		
23		

4.

n	$\frac{1}{2}n + 5$	$f(n)$
−2		
0		
2		
6		

Mathematics: Applications and Connections, Course 3

10-1 Practice

Functions

Complete each function table.

1. $f(n) = 9n$

n	9n	f(n)
−2		
−1		
0		
3		
4.5		

2. $f(n) = 3n - 5$

n	3n − 5	f(n)
−5		
0		
5		
10		
15		

3. $f(n) = n - 4$

n	n − 4	f(n)
−3		
−1		
0		
1		
3		

4. $f(n) = 6n + 3$

n	6n + 3	f(n)
−0.2		
0		
1		
0.4		
0.8		

5. $f(n) = 1.3n$

n	1.3n	f(n)
−2.3		
−1.7		
0.4		
1		
3		

6. $f(n) = -\frac{1}{4}n + 2$

n	$-\frac{1}{4}n + 2$	f(n)
−4		
−2		
0		
3.2		
8		

7. Find $f(-5)$ if $f(n) = 2n + 13$.

8. Find $f\left(\frac{1}{2}\right)$ if $f(n) = -3n - 8$.

9. Find $f(1.3)$ if $f(n) = 1.3n - 0.3$.

10. Find $f(-2.7)$ if $f(n) = -3n + 7$

Name _____ Date _____

10-2 Study Guide

Using Tables to Graph Functions

To graph a function, let the x-coordinate be the n value. Let the
y-coordinate be the $f(n)$ value.

Example   **Graph the function $f(n) = 2n + 2$.**
Make a table of values for n and find $f(n)$.
Then graph each ordered pair.

n	f(n)	(n, f(n))
−2	−2	(−2, −2)
0	2	(0, 2)
1	4	(1, 4)
2	6	(2, 6)

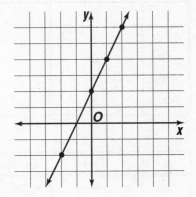

Complete each function table. Then graph the function.

1. $f(n) = 3n$

n	f(n)	(n, f(n))
−2		
−1		
0		
1		
2		

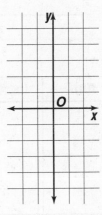

2. $f(n) = n + 4$

n	f(n)	(n, f(n))
−2		
−4		
0		
1		

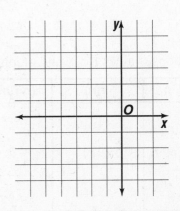

Mathematics: Applications and Connections, Course 3

10-2 Practice

Using Tables to Graph Functions

Complete each function table. Then graph the function.

1.

n	f(n)	(n, f(n))
−2	4	
−1	2	
0	0	
1	−2	
2	−4	

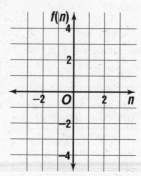

2.

n	f(n)	(n, f(n))
−2	4	
−1	1	
0	0	
1	1	
2	4	

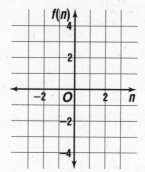

3. $f(n) = 2n - 2$

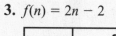

n	f(n)	(n, f(n))
0		
1		
2		
3		
4		

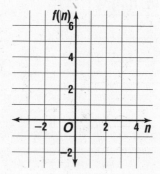

4. Choose values for n, and graph $f(n) = 0.5n + 2$.

n	f(n)	(n f(n))

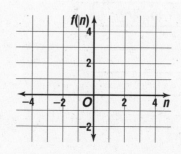

Mathematics: Applications and Connections, Course 3

10-3 Study Guide

Equations with Two Variables

The set of ordered pairs that make an equation true is the solution set for the equation.

Example **Find four solutions of $y = 1.5x + 2$. Write the solutions as a set of ordered pairs.**

Choose values for x.	Calculate y values.	Write ordered pairs.
Let $x = -3$.	$y = 1.5(-3) + 2$ or -2.5	$(-3, -2.5)$
Let $x = 0$.	$y = 1.5(0) + 2$ or 2	$(0, 2)$
Let $x = 2$.	$y = 1.5(2) + 2$ or 5	$(2, 5)$
Let $x = 5$.	$y = 1.5(5) + 2$ or 9.5	$(5, 9.5)$

Four solutions of the equation $y = 1.5x + 2$, are $\{(-3, -2.5), (0, 2), (2, 5), (5, 9.5)\}$.

Complete the table for each equation.

1. $y = 0.5x + 3$

x	y
−4	
0	
2	
10	

2. $y = -3x + 3$

x	y
−3	
0	
5	
10	

3. $y = \frac{x}{2} + 4$

x	y
−6	
−2	
4	
12	

Find four solutions of each equation.

4. $y = 4x - 2$

5. $y = -2x + 1$

6. $y = -2x + 5$

7. $y = -\frac{1}{2}x - 4$

8. $y = 2x + 3$

9. $y = 2.5x - 2$

Mathematics: Applications and Connections, Course 3

10-3 Practice

Equations with Two Variables

Complete the table for each equation.

1. $y = x + 2$

x	y
−2	
0	
1	
3	

2. $y = -2x$

x	y
−3	
−1	
5	
10	

3. $y = \frac{1}{2}x - 5$

x	y
−2	
0	
1	
3	

4. $y = 0.5x$

x	y
−4	
−1	
2	
8	

5. $y = 2x - 3$

x	y
−3	
−1	
0	
4	

6. $y = -3x + 2$

x	y
−3	
−1	
2	
4	

7. $y = 10x - 0.5$

x	y
−0.3	
−0.1	
0	
0.2	

8. $y = -0.5x + 1$

x	y
−2	
−1	
0	
5	

9. $y = \frac{1}{4}x + 4$

x	y
−8	
0	
4	
12	

Find four solutions of each equation.

10. $y = 2x - 1$

11. $y = -2x + 5$

Mathematics: Applications and Connections, Course 3

10-4 Study Guide

Graphing Linear Functions

An equation for which the graph of the solution is a straight line is a **linear function**.

Example Graph $y = 2x - 5$.

Make a function table.
List at least three values for x.

x	y	(x, y)
-1	-7	$(-1, -7)$
2	-1	$(2, -1)$
4	3	$(4, 3)$

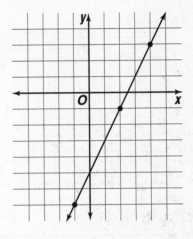

Graph the ordered pairs and connect them with a line.

Graph each function.

1. $y = 3x$

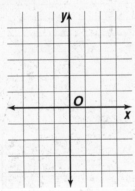

2. $y = \frac{x}{2} + 3$

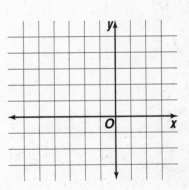

3. $y = 1.5x + 1$

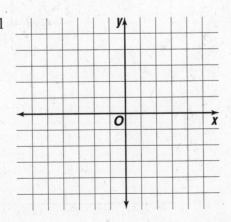

4. $y = -2x$

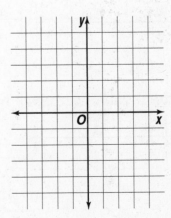

Mathematics: Applications and Connections, Course 3

10-4 Practice

Graphing Linear Functions

Complete each function table. Then graph the function.

1. $y = 2x$

x	y	(x, y)
-2		
-1		
0		
1		
2		

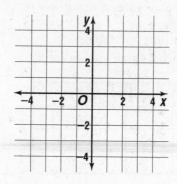

2. $y = 10 - x$

x	y	(x, y)
5		
7		
9		
10		
11		

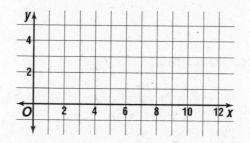

Graph each function.

3. $y = -3x$

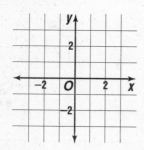

4. $y = 3x - 5$

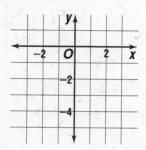

5. $y = 0.5x - 1.5$

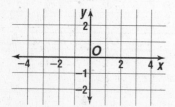

6. $y = 6 - \frac{1}{2}x$

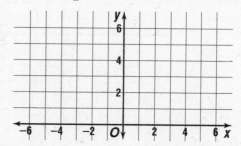

Mathematics: Applications and Connections, Course 3

10-5 Study Guide

Graphing Systems of Equations

If you graph two or more equations on the same coordinate plane, the point of intersection is the solution of the system of equations.

Example   **Graph the system of equations. Then find the solution of the system.**

$$y = x + 1$$
$$y = -2x + 4$$

Make a table for each equation.

$y = x + 1$ $y = -2x + 4$

x	y
-3	-2
0	1
3	4

x	y
-1	6
1	2
3	-2

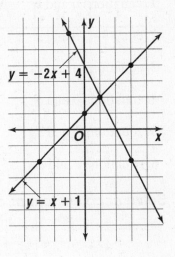

Graph each equation.

The lines intersect at the point (1, 2).
The solution to the system of equations is (1, 2).

Solve each system of equations by graphing.

1. $y = x + 2$
     $y = 2 - x$

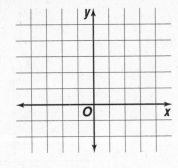

2. $y = -2x + 1$
     $y = x - 2$

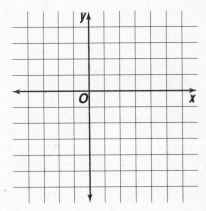

3. $y = x + 3$
     $y = 2x + 1$

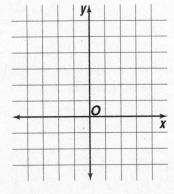

4. $y = -x + 1$
     $y = 2x + 4$

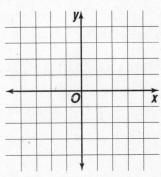

10-5 Practice

Graphing Systems of Equations

Lines a, b, c, and d are graphs of four equations. Use the graphs to find the solution to each system of equations.

1. equations *a* and *b*

2. equations *a* and *c*

3. equations *a* and *d*

4. equations *b* and *c*

5. equations *b* and *d*

6. equations *c* and *d*

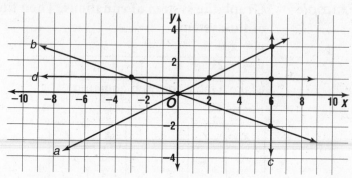

Solve each system of equations by graphing.

7. $y = 2x + 1$
   $y = 4x - 1$

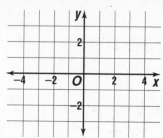

8. $y = -2x$
   $y = 3x$

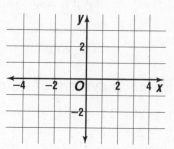

9. $y = 3x - 6$
   $y = -2x + 4$

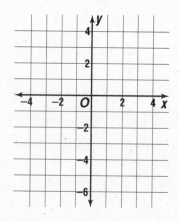

10. $y = x + 5$
    $y = -x + 1$

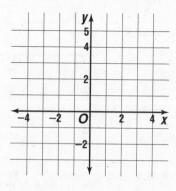

11. Find the solution for the system
    $y = \frac{1}{2}x + 7$ and $y = 3x + 2$.

12. Find the solution for the system
    $y - 2x = 1$ and $2x + y = -7$.

10-6 Study Guide

Graphing Quadratic Functions

A **quadratic function** contains a term with a power of 2. Graph a quadratic function the same way you graph a linear function.

Example   **Graph $y = -2x^2 + 5$.**

Make a function table.

x	y	(x, y)
-2	-3	(-2, -3)
-1	3	(-1, 3)
0	5	(0, 5)
1	3	(1, 3)
2	-3	(2, -3)

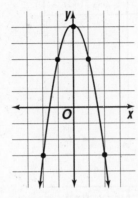

Graph the ordered pairs.
Connect the points with a smooth curve.

Graph each quadratic function.

1. $y = x^2 + 1$

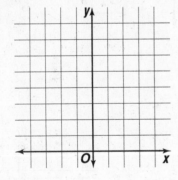

2. $y = 2x^2$

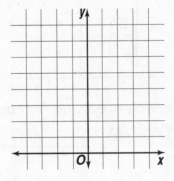

3. $y = -x^2 + 4$

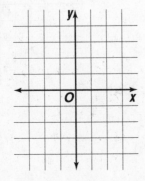

4. $y = 2x^2 - 4$

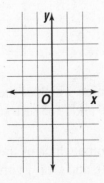

Mathematics: Applications and Connections, Course 3

Name_____ Date_____

Graphing Quadratic Functions

Complete each function table. Then graph the function.

1. $f(x) = 2x^2 - 3$

x	f(x)	(x, f(x))
−2		
−1		
0		
1		
2		

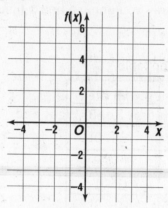

2. $f(x) = -\frac{1}{2}x^2$

x	f(x)	(x, f(x))
−2		
−1		
0		
1		
2		

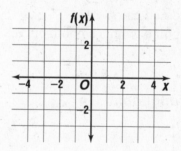

Graph each quadratic function.

3. $f(m) = -3m^2$

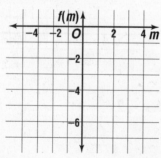

4. $y = x^2 - 2$

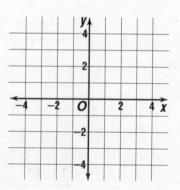

5. Determine which of the ordered pairs $(1, 6)$, $(2, 11)$, $(-4, 33)$, $(3, 21)$, and $(1, 5)$ are solutions for $y = 2x^2 + 3$.

6. Determine which of the ordered pairs $(0, 0)$, $(1, 0)$, $(-3, 6)$, $(-2, 6)$, and $(-1, 2)$ are solutions for $f(x) = x^2 - x$.

10-7 Study Guide

Integration: Geometry
Translations

To **translate** a figure in the direction described by an ordered pair, add the ordered pair to the coordinates of each vertex of the figure.

Example The vertices of $\triangle ABC$ are $A(-2, 2)$, $B(-1, -2)$, and $C(-6, 1)$. Graph the triangle. Then graph the triangle after a translation 7 units right and 3 units up.

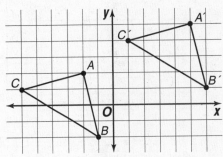

$A(-2, 2) + (7, 3) \longrightarrow A'(5, 5)$
$B(-1, -2) + (7, 3) \longrightarrow B'(6, 1)$
$C(-6, 1) + (7, 3) \longrightarrow C'(1, 4)$.

The vertices of the translated figure are $A'(5, 5)$, $B'(6, 1)$, and $C'(1, 4)$.

Graph $\triangle ABC$ and $\triangle A'B'C'$.

Find the coordinates of the vertices of each figure after the translation described. Then graph the figure and its translation.

1. $\triangle XYZ$ with vertices $X(-1, 2)$, $Y(2, 3)$, and $Z(3, -1)$, translated by $(-2, -3)$

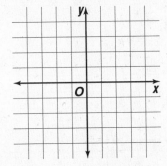

2. polygon $KLMN$ with vertices $K(-1, 1)$, $L(-3, 0)$, $M(-2, -3)$, $N(0, -2)$, translated by $(4, 3)$

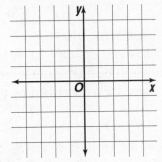

Find the coordinates of the vertices of each figure after the translation described.

3. $\triangle DEF$ with vertices $D(0, 5)$, $E(-1, 3)$, and $F(-3, 4)$, translated by $(2, -1)$

4. pentagon $ABCDE$ with vertices $A(4, -1)$, $B(3, 2)$, $C(1, 4)$, $D(-2, 1)$, and $E(-3, -3)$, translated by $(-2, 1)$

Practice

Integration: Geometry
Translations

**Name the coordinates of the ordered pair needed to translate
each point A to point B.**

1.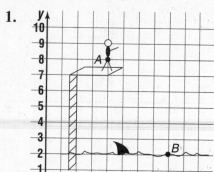

2.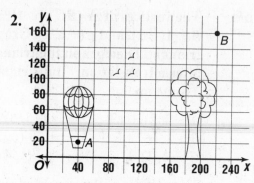

3. Translate △ABC with vertices A(−1, 4), B(0, 0),
   and C(2, 3) by (5, −2). Then graph △A′B′C′.

   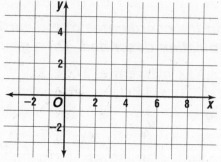

4. Rectangle QRST has vertices Q(−1, −2), R(−2, 1), S(4, 3),
   and T(5, 0). Find the coordinates of the vertices of
   Q′R′S′T′ after a translation described by (1, −2).

5. The coordinates of the vertices of △ABC
   are A(3, −1), B(0, 2) and C(3, −2). Find the
   coordinates of the vertices of △A′B′C′, which
   is △ABC translated by (−3, −2). Then graph
   △ABC and its translation.

   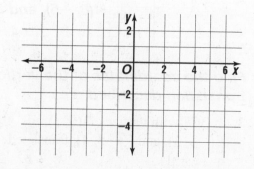

6. Square ABCD has vertex A(−5, −12). When translated,
   A′ has coordinates (6, 10). Describe the translation using
   an ordered pair.

*Mathematics: Applications
and Connections, Course 3*

10-8 Study Guide

Integration: Geometry
Reflections

When a figure is **reflected** on a coordinate plane, every point of the figure has a corresponding point on the other side of the line of symmetry.

To reflect a figure over the x-axis, use the same x-coordinate and multiply the y-coordinate by -1.

To reflect a figure over the y-axis, multiply the x-coordinate by -1 and use the same y-coordinate.

Example $\triangle ABC$ has vertices
$A(-2, -2)$, $B(-5, -4)$, $C(-1, -5)$.

$\triangle ABC$ reflected over the x-axis
has vertices at $(-2, 2)$, $(-5, 4)$, $(-1, 5)$.

$\triangle ABC$ reflected over the y-axis
has vertices at $(2, -2)$, $(5, -4)$, $(1, -5)$.

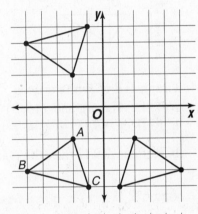

Graph trapezoid BIRD with vertices
B(1, 1), I(2, 4), R(6, 4), and D(7, 1).

1. Find the coordinates of the vertices
   after a reflection over the x-axis.
   Graph the reflection.

2. Find the coordinates of the vertices
   after a reflection over the y-axis.
   Graph the reflection.

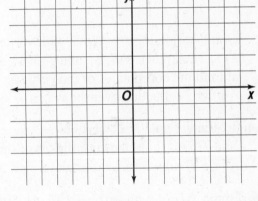

Graph parallelogram JUNE with vertices
J(2, −2), U(6, −2), N(8, −5), and E(4, −5).

3. Find the coordinates of the vertices
   after a reflection over the x-axis.
   Graph the reflection.

4. Find the coordinates of the vertices
   after a reflection over the y-axis.
   Graph the reflection.

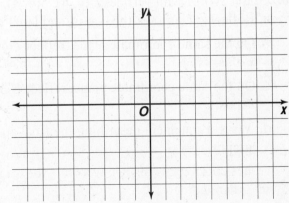

*Mathematics: Applications
and Connections*, Course 3

Name_____ Date_____

10-8 Practice

Integration: Geometry
Reflections

Name the line of symmetry for each pair of figures.

1.

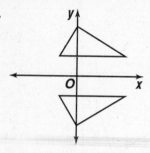

2.

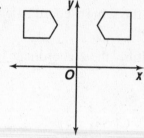

3.

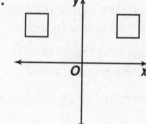

4. Graph △BAT with vertices
   B(1, 1), A(2, 3), and T(5, 3)
   a. Reflect △BAT over the x-axis.

   b. Reflect △BAT over the y-axis.

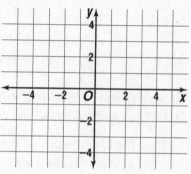

5. Graph parallelogram KENT with vertices
   K(1, 2), E(5, 4), N(7, 3), and T(3, 1).
   a. Find the coordinates of the vertices
   after a reflection over the y-axis.

   b. Graph the parallelogram K'E'N'T'.

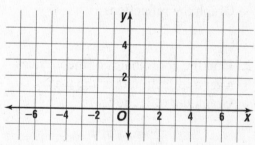

6. Graph △USA with vertices U(0, 4), S(4, 4), and A(4, 0).
   a. Reflect △USA over the y-axis, and label U'S'A'.

   b. On the same coordinate plane, reflect △USA over the
   x-axis.

   c. On the same coordinate plane, reflect U'S'A' over the
   x-axis.

   d. Write a statement describing the final appearance of the four
   graphs.

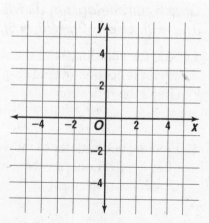

*Mathematics: Applications
and Connections*, Course 3

10-9 Study Guide

Integration: Geometry Rotations

Triangle *XYZ* has vertices *X*(−4, 1), *Y*(−1, 5), and *Z*(−6, 9).

To **rotate** △*XYZ* 180°, multiply each coordinate by −1.

$(-4, 1) \rightarrow (4, -1)$
$(-1, 5) \rightarrow (1, -5)$
$(-6, 9) \rightarrow (6, -9)$

To rotate △*XYZ* 90° counterclockwise, switch the coordinates and multiply the first by −1.

$(-4, 1) \rightarrow (-1, -4)$
$(-1, 5) \rightarrow (-5, -1)$
$(-6, 9) \rightarrow (-9, -6)$

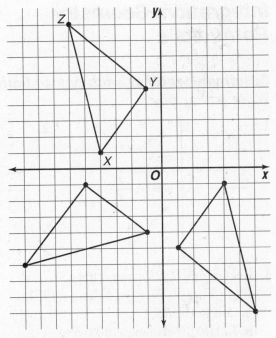

Triangle RST has vertices R(−2, −1), S(0, −4), and Y(−4, −7).

1. Graph △*RST*.

2. Find the coordinates of the vertices after a 90° counterclockwise rotation. Graph the rotation.

3. Find the coordinates of the vertices after a 180° rotation. Graph the rotation.

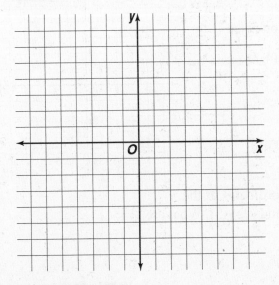

Rectangle TWIN has vertices T(2, 1), W(6, 3), I(5, 5), and N(1, 3).

4. Graph rectangle *TWIN*.

5. Find the coordinates of the vertices after a 90° counterclockwise rotation. Graph the rotation.

6. Find the coordinates of the vertices after a 180° rotation. Graph the rotation.

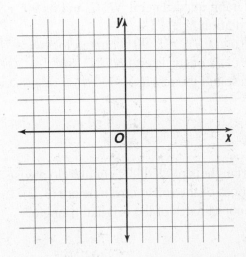

Mathematics: Applications and Connections, Course 3

Name _____ **Date** _____

10-9 Practice

Integration: Geometry
Rotations

Determine whether each pair of figures represents a rotation. Write yes or no.

1.

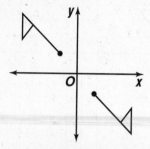

2.

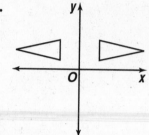

3.

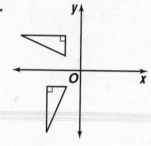

4. Rectangle *WORK* has vertices
   $W(1, 3)$, $O(4, 6)$, $R(6, 4)$, and $K(3, 1)$.
   a. Graph *WORK*.
   b. Rotate the rectangle 90°
   counterclockwise, and graph $W'O'R'K'$.
   c. Rotate the rectangle 180°, and graph $W''O''R''K''$.

5. Examine the figure at the right.
   a. Does the figure have rotational
   symmetry?
   b. If so, find the degree turns that
   show this symmetry.

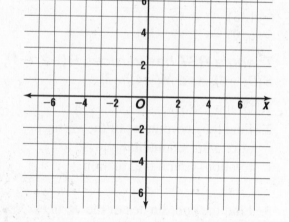

6. Quadrilateral *NEAL* has vertices $N(3, 5)$,
   $E(4, 4)$, $A(3, 2)$ and $L(1, 3)$.
   a. Graph quadrilateral *NEAL* and its 90° counterclockwise
   rotation $N'E'A'L'$.
   b. Rotate $N'E'A'L'$ 90° counterclockwise.
   c. Rotate quadrilateral *NEAL* 180°.
   Explain the result.

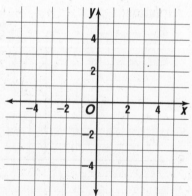

7. A triangle is rotated 90° counterclockwise. The coordinates of the
   vertices of the rotated triangle are $(3, 2)$, $(-1, 3)$, and $(2, -3)$. What are
   the coordinates of the original triangle?

*Mathematics: Applications
and Connections, Course 3*

11-1 Study Guide

Area of Circles

The area (A) of a circle equals π times the radius (r) squared: $A = \pi r^2$.

Examples   **1** **Find the area of the circle.**

$A = \pi r^2$

$A \approx 3.14 \left(\frac{13}{2}\right)^2$ *Use 3.14 for π.*

$A \approx 3.14(42.25)$

$A \approx 132.665$

The area of the circle is about 132.7 in².

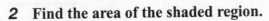

2 **Find the area of the shaded region.**

Find the area of   Find the area of
the large circle.   a small circle.

$A = \pi r^2$ $A = \pi r^2$

$A \approx 3.14(20)^2$ $A \approx 3.14(6)^2$

$A \approx 1256$ $A \approx 113.04$

Now find the area of the shaded region.

$A \approx 1256 - 3(113.04)$

$\approx 1256 - 339.12$

≈ 916.88

The area of the shaded region is about 916.9 m².

Find the area of each circle to the nearest tenth.

1.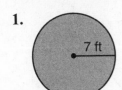
7 ft

2.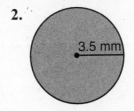
3.5 mm

3.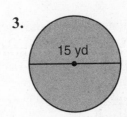
15 yd

Find the area of each shaded region to the nearest tenth.

4.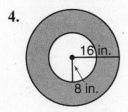
16 in.
8 in.

5.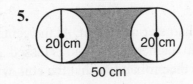
20 cm   20 cm
50 cm

6.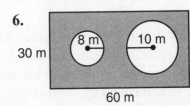
8 m   10 m
30 m
60 m

11-1 Practice

Area of Circles

Find the area of each circle to the nearest tenth.

1. 10 ft

2. 14 in.

3. 5 cm

4. 6.3 m

5. 24 ft

6. 5 ft

7. Find the area of a circle that has a diameter of 60 feet.

8. Find the area of a circle that has a radius of 22 feet.

9. Find the diameter of a circle that has an area of 36π square inches.

Find the area of each shaded region to the nearest tenth.

10. 3 ft   5 ft

11. 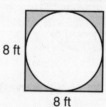 8 ft   8 ft

12. 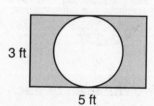 3 ft   5 ft

13. A circular flower garden has a diameter of 16 feet. At the center of the garden is a circular pool 5 feet in diameter. If a coin is tossed at random into the garden, what is the probability that the coin will land in the pool?

Mathematics: Applications and Connections, Course 3

11-2 Study Guide

Three-Dimensional Figures

Prisms have at least one pair of faces that are parallel and congruent. These are called **bases. Pyramids** have a polygon for a base and triangles for sides. Prisms and pyramids are named by the shape of their bases.

Example   **Use isometric dot paper to sketch a hexagonal prism that is 5 units long.**

Step 1   Lightly draw a hexagon for a base.

Step 2   Lightly draw the vertical segments at the vertices of the base. Each segment is 5 units high.

Step 3   Complete the top of the prism.

Step 4   Go over your lines. Use dashed lines for the edges of the prism you cannot see from your perspective and solid lines for the edges you can see.

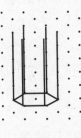

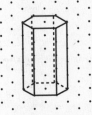

Use isometric dot paper to draw each solid.

1. a rectangular prism that is 2 units high, 5 units long, and 3 units wide

2. a pentagonal prism that is 3 units high

3. a square pyramid with a base that is 4 units wide

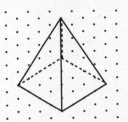

Name each solid.

4.

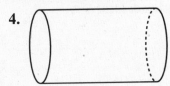

5.

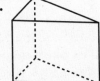

6.

     Mathematics: Applications and Connections, Course 3

11-2 Practice

Three-Dimensional Figures

Solve.

1. What are the dimensions of the prism shown at the right?

2. What is the height of the prism?

3. What type of prism is this?

4. Draw another view of this prism showing a height of 1 unit.

5. Draw another view of this prism showing a height of 3 units.

6. Draw a view of a prism that has a triangle as a base, and is 4 units high.

7. Draw a view of a prism that has a pentagon for a base.

8. Draw a view of a cone.

9. Draw a bird's-eye view of the cone in Exercise 8 as it would appear from directly overhead. Describe the bird's-eye view.

10. What is the greatest number of cubes with a one-inch edge that can be cut from a cube that has a three-inch edge?

Mathematics: Applications and Connections, Course 3

11-3 Study Guide

Volume of Prisms and Cylinders

The volume (V) of a prism is the area of the base (B) times the height (h): $V = Bh$.

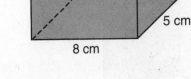

4 cm

5 cm

8 cm

Example 1 Find the volume of the rectangular prism.

$$V = \ell wh$$
$$V = 4 \times 5 \times 8$$
$$V = 160$$

The volume of the rectangular prism is 160 cubic centimeters.

The volume (V) of a cylinder is the area of the base (B) times the height (h). Since the area of the base $= \pi r^2$, the volume of the cylinder may be expressed as $V = \pi r^2 h$.

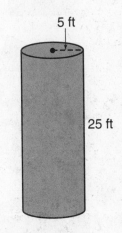

5 ft

25 ft

Example 2 Find the volume of the cylinder.

$$V = \pi r^2 h$$
$$V \approx 3.14(5)^2(12)$$
$$V \approx 3.14(25)(12)$$
$$V \approx 942$$

The volume of the cylinder is 942 cubic feet.

Find the volume of each solid to the nearest tenth.

1.
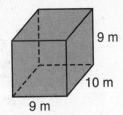
9 m
10 m
9 m

2.
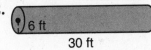
6 ft
30 ft

3.
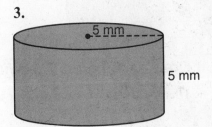
5 mm
5 mm

4.
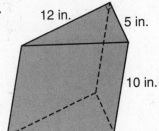
12 in.
5 in.
10 in.

5.
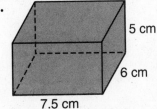
5 cm
6 cm
7.5 cm

6.
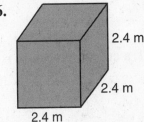
2.4 m
2.4 m
2.4 m

Mathematics: Applications and Connections, Course 3

11-3 Practice

Volume of Prisms and Cylinders

Find the volume of each solid to the nearest tenth.

1.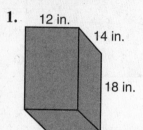
12 in.
14 in.
18 in.

2.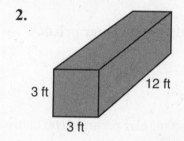
3 ft
12 ft
3 ft

3.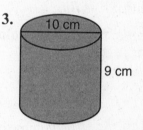
10 cm
9 cm

4.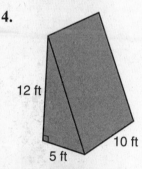
12 ft
10 ft
5 ft

5.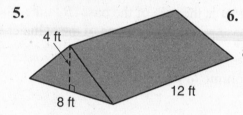
4 ft
8 ft
12 ft

6.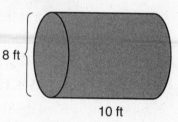
8 ft
10 ft

7.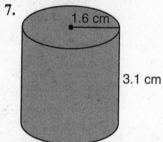
1.6 cm
3.1 cm

8.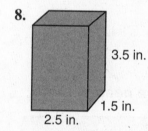
3.5 in.
1.5 in.
2.5 in.

9.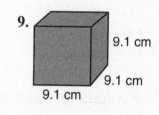
9.1 cm
9.1 cm
9.1 cm

Draw each figure. Then find its volume to the nearest tenth.

10. a cylinder whose diameter is 6 cm and whose height is 4 cm

11. a cube whose edge is 3.5 inches

Mathematics: Applications and Connections, Course 3

11-4 Study Guide

Volume of Pyramids and Cones

The volume (V) of a cone equals one-third the area of the base (B) times the height (h). Since the area of the base is πr^2, the volume of a cone may be expressed as $V = \frac{1}{3}\pi r^2 h$.

Example 1   **Find the volume of the cone.**

$V = \frac{1}{3}\pi r^2 h$

$V \approx \frac{1}{3}(3.14)(9)^2(20)$

$V \approx \frac{1}{3}(3.14)(81)(20)$

$V \approx 1,695.6$

The volume of the cone is about 1,695.6 cubic feet.

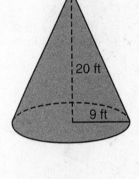

The volume (V) of a pyramid equals one-third the area of the base (B) times the height (h): $V = \frac{1}{3}Bh$.

Example 2   **Find the volume of the square pyramid.**

$V = \frac{1}{3}Bh$

$V = \frac{1}{3}s^2 h$ *Since the base is a square, $B = s^2$.*

$V = \frac{1}{3}(3.6)^2(9)$

$V = \frac{1}{3}(12.96)(9)$

$V = 38.88$

The volume of the pyramid is 38.88 cubic meters.

Find the volume of each solid to the nearest tenth.

1.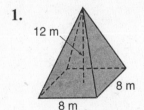

2.

3.

4.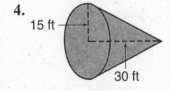

5.

6.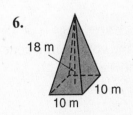

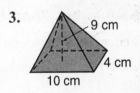

Mathematics: Applications and Connections, Course 3

11-4 Practice

Volume of Pyramids and Cones

Find the volume of each solid to the nearest tenth.

1.
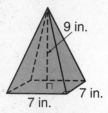
9 in.
7 in.
7 in.

2.
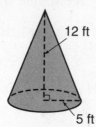
12 ft
5 ft

3.
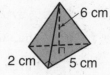
6 cm
2 cm
5 cm

4.
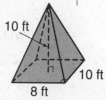
7 ft
3 ft

5.
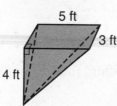
5 ft
3 ft
4 ft

6.
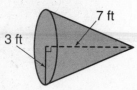
8 in.
10 in.

7.
10 ft
10 ft
8 ft

8.
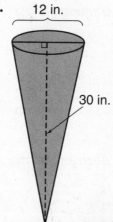
12 in.
30 in.

9.
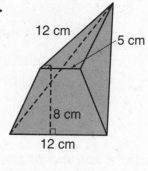
12 cm
5 cm
8 cm
12 cm

10. Find the volume of a pyramid whose base area is 12 cm^2 and whose height is 11 cm.

11. Find the volume of a cone whose base area is 45.6 in^2 and whose height is 8 in.

11-5 Study Guide

Surface Area of Prisms

The **surface area** of a prism is equal to the sum of the areas of its faces.

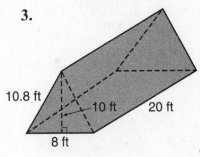

8 cm 20 cm 6 cm 10 cm

Example   **Find the surface area of the triangular prism.**

Find the area of each of the faces.

base	$b = 6, h = 8$	$A = \frac{1}{2}bh$	$A = \frac{1}{2}(6)(8)$ or 24
base	$b = 6, h = 8$	$A = \frac{1}{2}bh$	$A = \frac{1}{2}(6)(8)$ or 24
face	$\ell = 20, w = 6$	$A = \ell w$	$A = 20(6)$ or 120
face	$\ell = 20, w = 8$	$A = \ell w$	$A = 20(8)$ or 160
face	$\ell = 20, w = 10$	$A = \ell w$	$A = 20(10)$ or 200

Add to find the total surface area: $24 + 24 + 120 + 160 + 200 = 528$.

The surface area of the prism is 528 square centimeters.

Find the surface area of each prism to the nearest tenth.

1.

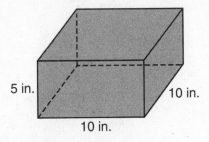

5 in.   10 in.   10 in.

2.

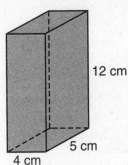

12 cm   5 cm   4 cm

3.

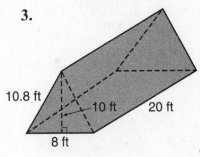

10.8 ft   10 ft   20 ft   8 ft

4.

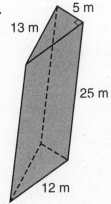

5 m   13 m   25 m   12 m

5.

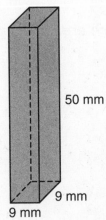

50 mm   9 mm   9 mm

6.

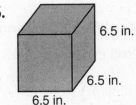

6.5 in.   6.5 in.   6.5 in.

Mathematics: Applications and Connections, Course 3

11-5 Practice

Surface Area of Prisms

Identify each prism. Then find its surface area.

1.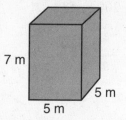

11 ft
11 ft
11 ft

2.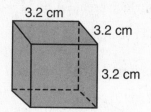

10 in.
6 in.
8 in.
10 in.

3.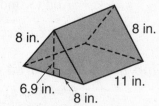

1 cm
5 cm
10 cm

Find the surface area of each prism to the nearest tenth.

4.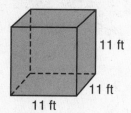

7 m
5 m
5 m

5.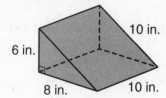

3.2 cm
3.2 cm
3.2 cm

6.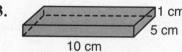

8 in.
8 in.
8 in.
6.9 in.
8 in.
11 in.

7.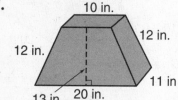

10 in.
12 in.
12 in.
11 in
13 in.
20 in.

8.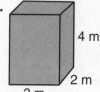

4 m
2 m
3 m

9.

5 cm
13 cm
12 cm
8 cm

Draw each figure. Then find its surface area.

10. a rectangular prism with a length of 5 feet, a height of 8 feet, and a width of 3 feet

11. a cube having edges of $3\frac{1}{2}$ inches

Mathematics: Applications and Connections, Course 3

11-6 Study Guide

Surface Area of Cylinders

The surface area of a cylinder is equal to the sum of the areas of the two circular bases plus the area of the rectangle that forms the curved side. The length of the rectangle is equal to the circumference of the base.

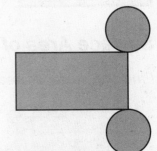

Example   **Find the surface area of the cylinder.**

area of each base: $A = \pi r^2$
$A \approx 3.14(8)^2$
$A \approx 3.14(64)$
$A \approx 200.96$

area of the rectangle: $A = \ell w$
$A = 2\pi(r)(w)$
$A \approx 2(3.14)(8)(20)$
$A \approx 6.28(160)$
$A \approx 1,004.8$

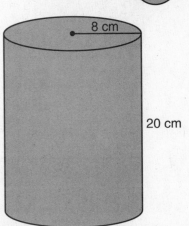

The total surface area is about $200.96 + 200.96 + 1,004.8$ or $1,406.72$. The surface area of the cylinder is about $1,406.72$ square centimeters.

Find the surface area of each cylinder to the nearest tenth.

1.

24 m

4 m

2.

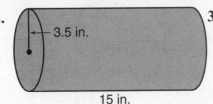

3.5 in.

15 in.

3.

10 cm

10 cm

Draw each cylinder. Then find its surface area to the nearest tenth.

4. The radius of the base is 5 inches.
The height is 10 inches.

5. The diameter of the base is 6 centimeters. The height is 12 centimeters.

11-6 Practice

Surface Area of Cylinders

Find the surface area of each cylinder to the nearest tenth.

1.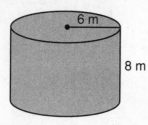
6 m
8 m

2.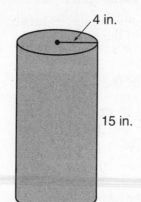
4 in.
15 in.

3.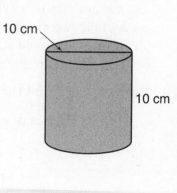
10 cm
10 cm

4.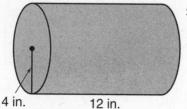
4 in.   12 in.

5.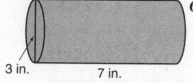
3 in.   7 in.

6.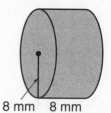
8 mm   8 mm

7.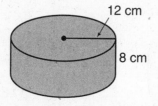
12 cm
8 cm

8.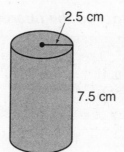
2.5 cm
7.5 cm

9.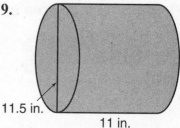
11.5 in.
11 in.

Draw each cylinder. Then find its surface area.

10. The radius of the base is 4 inches, and the height is 10 inches.

11. The diameter of the base is 20 centimeters, and the height is 20 centimeters.

11-7 Study Guide

Integration: Measurement
Precision and Significant Digits

The smaller the unit of measure, the more **precise** the measurement.

Example 1 **Which is more precise, 38 mm or 4 cm? 40 mm or 4 cm?**

> 38 mm is more precise because the millimeter is a smaller unit of measure. 40 mm and 4 cm have the same precision.

Significant digits are those digits that correctly represent the accuracy of the measurement. If a zero does not fall between two significant digits and is only a placeholder for locating the decimal point, it is not a significant digit.

Number	Significant Digits	Number	Significant Digits
14.5	3	85,000	2
145,224	6	0.0009	1
10.08	4	15.0020	5

The **greatest possible error** is half the smallest unit used to make the measurement. The **relative error** is the quotient of the greatest possible error and the measurement itself.

Example 2 **Analyze the measurement 0.0763 centimeter.**

- The length is measured to the nearest 0.0001 centimeter.
- There are 3 significant digits.
- The greatest possible error is $\frac{0.0001}{2}$ or 0.00005 centimeter.
- The relative error is $\frac{0.00005}{0.0763}$ or about 0.00066.

Analyze each measurement. Give the precision, significant digits, greatest possible error, and relative error to two significant digits.

1. 7.06 km

2. 18,000 people

3. 0.003 in.

4. 50.007 seconds

5. $123,000.00

6. 4,672 feet

Mathematics: Applications and Connections, Course 3

11-7 Practice

Integration: Measurement
Precision and Significant Digits

*Analyze each measurement. Give the precision, significant
digits if appropriate, greatest possible error, and relative error
to two significant digits.*

1. 4.06 ft

2. 3,500 ft

3. 28.6 cm

4. 0.0123g

5. 41 in.

6. 6 mi

7. 5.38 in.

8. 0.205 m

9. 5.0010 cm

10. 0.300 cm

11. 2,600 ft

12. 400 mi

13. 401 ft

14. 401.0 ft

15. 35.9 m

16. Which is the more precise measurement for the capacity of a
container, $3\frac{1}{2}$ gallons or 450 ounces?

17. Which is the more precise measurement for the height of a person,
$73\frac{1}{2}$ inches or 6 feet?

18. How many significant digits are in the measure 0.0003 cm?

19. How many significant digits are in the measure 0.0203 cm?

12-1 Study Guide

Counting Outcomes

You can draw a **tree diagram** to find the number of possible combinations or outcomes.

Example   Windbreaker jackets come in red, blue, or green and in
sizes small, medium, and large. How many possible
combinations are there?

Color	Size	Combination
	small	red, small
red	medium	red, medium
	large	red, large
	small	blue, small
blue	medium	blue, medium
	large	blue, large
	small	green, small
green	medium	green, medium
	large	green, large

The Fundamental Counting Principle says: If event M can occur in m ways
and it is followed by event N that can occur in n ways, then the event M
followed by event N can occur in mn ways.

The number of possible combinations for the example above is:

number of colors		number of sizes		possible combinations
3	$\times$	3	$=$	9

Draw a tree diagram to find the number of possible outcomes for each situation.

1. You have a choice of vanilla,
blueberry, or chocolate ice cream on
a sugar or regular cone.

2. You toss three coins.

State the number of possible outcomes for each event.

3. Two dice are rolled.

4. Shirts come in 4 colors and 3 sizes.

5. You have a choice of 6 entrees and 4
desserts.

6. A test consists of 5 true or false
questions.

Name_____ Date_____

12-1 Practice

Counting Outcomes

1. Three coins are tossed and a die is rolled.

   a. Draw a tree diagram that represents the situation.

   b. How many outcomes are possible?

   c. How many outcomes show 3 tails?

   d. How many outcomes show a 6 on the die?

   e. How many show 3 heads and a 3 on the die?

   f. What is the probability of exactly 1 head and an even number on the die?

2. A quiz has eight true-false questions. How many outcomes for giving answers to the eight questions are possible?

Draw a tree diagram to find the number of possible outcomes for each situation.

3. A coin is tossed, then a die is tossed, then another coin is tossed.

4. This spinner is spun twice.

State the number of possible outcomes for each event.

5. three dice are rolled

6. three coins are tossed

7. Canned beans are packed in 3 sizes: small, medium, and large; and are red, black-eyed, green, yellow, or baked.

8. A confectioner offers milk, dark, or white chocolates with solid, cream, jelly, nut, fruit, or caramel centers.

Mathematics: Applications and Connections, Course 3

12-2 Study Guide

Permutations

An arrangement or listing in which order is important is called a **permutation**.

Example 1   **5 people are running a race. How many arrangements of winner, second place, and third place are possible?**

There are 5 choices for winner.
Then, there are 4 choices for second place.
Finally, there are 3 possible choices for third place.

$5 \times 4 \times 3 = 60$

There are 60 permutations.

For the example above, the permutation of 5 runners taken 3 at a time may be written: $P(5, 3) = 5 \times 4 \times 3$.

The product of counting numbers beginning at n and counting backward to 1 is called n factorial. n factorial is written $n!$.

Example 2   **In how many different ways can 6 people stand in a row?**

$P(6, 6) = 6!$
$\quad\quad\quad = 6 \times 5 \times 4 \times 3 \times 2 \times 1$
$\quad\quad\quad = 720$

6 people can stand in a row 720 different ways.

Find each value.

1. $P(4, 2)$ **2.** $P(7, 3)$ **3.** $P(10, 4)$ **4.** $P(5, 5)$

5. 3!   **6.** 8!   **7.** 1!   **8.** 5!

In how many different ways can the letters of each word be arranged?

9. SUN   **10.** RAIN   **11.** CLOUDS   **12.** WINDY

12-2 Practice

Permutations

Find each value.

1. $P(6, 2)$ **2.** $P(8, 3)$ **3.** $4!$ **4.** $8!$

5. $0!$ **6.** $P(7, 4)$ **7.** $P(4, 2)$ **8.** $1!$

9. $5!$ **10.** $P(3, 2)$ **11.** $P(9, 9)$ **12.** $9!$

How many different ways can the letters of each word be arranged?

13. BUY   **14.** BROUGHT   **15.** BREAK   **16.** PENCIL

17. How many odd four-digit numbers can be formed from the digits 1, 2, 3, and 4? Write the possible odd numbers.

18. How many even four-digit numbers can be formed from the digits 1, 2, 3 and 5? Write the possible even numbers.

19. In how many different ways can you arrange the letters in the word JOURNALISM if you take the letters six at a time?
a. Write the number of permutations in the form $P(n, r)$.

b. Write the number as a decimal numeral.

94   *Mathematics: Applications and Connections, Course 3*

12-3 Study Guide

Combinations

Arrangements or listings in which order is not important are called **combinations**.

Example   **In how many ways can 3 representatives be chosen from a group of 12 people?**

$C(12, 3)$ means the number of combinations of 12 things taken 3 at a time.

$$C(12, 3) = \frac{P(12, 3)}{3!}$$

Divide by 3! to eliminate combinations that are the same.

$$= \frac{12 \times 11 \times 10}{3 \times 2 \times 1}$$

$$= \frac{1,320}{6} \text{ or } 220$$

3 representatives can be chosen from a group of 12 people in 220 ways.

Find each value.

1. $C(6, 3)$ **2.** $C(10, 4)$ **3.** $C(9, 2)$ **4.** $C(5, 5)$

5. In how many ways can a starting team of 5 players be chosen from a team of 14 players?

6. For a history test, students are asked to write essays on 4 topics from a list of 9 topics. How many different combinations are possible?

7. How many different 2-card hands are possible from a deck of 52 cards?

8. In how many ways can a delegation of 4 students be chosen from a class of 22 students?

12-3 Practice

Combinations

Find each value.

1. $C(4, 2)$

2. $C(5, 3)$

3. $C(6, 2)$

4. $C(7, 3)$

5. $C(6, 4)$

6. $C(7, 7)$

7. $C(12, 8)$

8. $C(15, 6)$

9. $C(15, 8)$

Determine whether each situation is a permutation or a combination.

10. 2 drinking glasses from 6 on a shelf

11. 6 drinking glasses on a shelf

12. 4 cards from a 52-card deck

13. 3 numbers from 1 to 9

14. How many different four-digit numbers can be written using the digits 0, 1, 2, 3, 4, and 5 only once in each number?

15. How many ways can you choose four toy soldiers from a collection of sixteen toy soldiers?

16. How many different five-card hands are possible using a 52-card deck?

17. How many combinations of four textbooks can be chosen from eight textbooks in a locker?

18. How many different "double features" (two-film showings) can be chosen from a collection of twelve films?

12-4 Study Guide

Pascal's Triangle

You can use **Pascal's Triangle** to solve problems about combinations.

Row 0	1
Row 1	1 1
Row 2	1 2 1
Row 3	1 3 3 1
Row 4	1 4 6 4 1
Row 5	1 5 10 10 5 1
Row 6	1 6 15 20 15 6 1
Row 7	1 7 21 35 35 21 7 1

Example **How many combinations are possible for 7 things taken 3 at a time?**

Since there are 7 things, use row 7. Find the number that matches 3 things taken at a time.

Row 7	1	7	21	35	35	21	7	1
Taken at a time	0	1	2	3	4	5	6	7

From the triangle, there are 35 combinations of 7 things taken 3 at a time.

Use Pascal's Triangle to find each value.

1. $C(3, 2)$ 2. $C(7, 6)$ 3. $C(4, 1)$ 4. $C(5, 2)$

Use Pascal's Triangle to answer each question.

5. How many combinations are possible when 5 things are taken 4 at a time?

6. How many possible 5-person starting teams can be formed from a 7-person squad?

7. In how many different ways can 3 golf clubs be selected from 6 golf clubs?

12-4 Practice

Pascal's Triangle

Use Pascal's Triangle to find each value.

1. $C(3, 2)$ 2. $C(4, 3)$ 3. $C(4, 2)$ 4. $C(5, 3)$

5. $C(6, 2)$ 6. $C(6, 3)$ 7. $C(7, 4)$ 8. $C(8, 5)$

Use Pascal's Triangle to answer each question.

9. Write the next four rows.

10. **a.** What is the second number in row 3?

   b. What is the second number in row 9?

   c. What is the second number in row n?

```
                1
              1   1
            1   2   1
          1   3   3   1
        1   4   6   4   1
      1   5  10  10   5   1
    1   6  15  20  15   6   1
  1   7  21  35  35  21   7   1
1   8  28  56  70  56  28   8   1
1  9  36  84 126 126  84  36   9   1
```

11. How many different pizza varieties are possible:
   a. if 5 toppings are offered?   **b.** if 7 toppings are offered

12. If there are two true-false questions on a quiz, what does the "2" in row two mean?

13. If there are four true-false questions on a quiz, what do the 1s in row four mean?

14. How many different ways can a quiz with eight true-false questions be answered?

15. Four coins are tossed.
   a. What is the probability that all four will be heads?
   b. What is the probability that there will be two heads and two tails?
   c. What is the probability that at least one will be a head?

12-5 Study Guide

Probability of Compound Events

If the outcome of one event does not affect the outcome of a second even, the two events are **independent.** The probability of two independent events can be found by multiplying the probability of the first event by the probability of the second event: $P(A \text{ and } B) = P(A) \times P(B)$.

Example 1   **A die is rolled and a coin is tossed. Find the probability of getting an odd number and a tail.**

$P(\text{odd number}) = \frac{1}{2}$ $P(\text{tail}) = \frac{1}{2}$

$P(\text{odd number and tail}) = \frac{1}{2} \times \frac{1}{2} \text{ or } \frac{1}{4}$

The probability of getting an odd number and a tail is $\frac{1}{4}$.

If the outcome of one event affects the outcome of a second event, the two events are **dependent.** The probability of two dependent events can be found by multiplying: $P(A \text{ and } B) = P(A) \times P(B)$.

Example 2   **There are 6 black socks and 4 white socks in a drawer. If one is taken out without looking and then a second is taken out, what is the probability they will both be black?**

$P(\text{first sock black}) = \frac{6}{10} \text{ or } \frac{3}{5}$ *After the first draw, there are*
9 socks left and 5 are black.
$P(\text{second sock black}) = \frac{5}{9}$

$P(\text{two black socks}) = \frac{3}{5} \times \frac{5}{9}$

$\qquad\qquad\qquad\quad = \frac{1}{3}$

The probability of choosing two black socks is $\frac{1}{3}$.

A card is drawn from a deck numbered 1 through 10 and a die is rolled. Find the probability of each outcome.

1. a 10 and a 3   2. two even numbers   3. two prime numbers

4. two odd numbers   5. an even number and a prime   6. a 7 and a 5

There are 4 red pencils, 6 green pencils, and 5 yellow pencils in a jar. Once a pencil is selected, it is not replaced. Find the probability of each outcome.

7. a red and a yellow   8. two green   9. a green and a yellow

12-5 Practice

Probability of Compound Events

A die is rolled and the spinner is spun. Find each probability.

1. $P(1 \text{ and } A)$
2. $P(\text{odd and } B)$

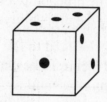

3. $P(\text{composite and } C)$ 4. $P(\text{prime and } D)$

5. $P(1 \text{ and } E)$
6. Why are these independent events?

In a bag there are 3 red marbles, 2 yellow marbles, and 1 blue marble. Once a marble is selected, it is not replaced. Find the probability of each outcome.

7. a red marble and then a yellow marble

8. a blue marble and then a yellow marble

9. a red marble and then a blue marble

10. any color marble except yellow and then a yellow marble

11. a red marble three times in a row

In a bag there are 3 red marbles, 2 yellow marbles, and 1 blue marble. After a marble is selected, it is replaced. Using this new situation, find the probability of each outcome listed above.

12. Exercise 7
13. Exercise 8
14. Exercise 9

15. Exercise 10
16. Exercise 11

Each spinner is spun once. Find each probability.

17. 2 and B
18. even number and C

19. odd number and vowel
20. prime number and D

12-6 Study Guide

Experimental Probability

Probabilities determined by conducting an experiment are **experimental probabilities.**

Example   Yolanda drew one card from a 52-card deck, tallied its suit, and returned the card to the deck. She performed the experiment 100 times. The chart shows the results.

	Heart	Club	Diamond	Spade
Tally	~~HHT~~ ~~HHT~~ ~~HHT~~ ~~HHT~~ ~~HHT~~ ~~HHT~~ ~~HHT~~ ~~HHT~~ ~~HHT~~ II	~~HHT~~ ~~HHT~~ ~~HHT~~ ~~HHT~~ II	~~HHT~~ ~~HHT~~ ~~HHT~~ II	~~HHT~~ ~~HHT~~ ~~HHT~~ ~~HHT~~ ~~HHT~~ ~~HHT~~ IIII
Total	32	22	17	29

Yolanda's experimental probability of drawing a heart is $\frac{32}{100}$ or $\frac{8}{25}$.

Since there are 52 cards and 13 of them are hearts, the theoretical probability of drawing a heart is $\frac{13}{52}$ or $\frac{1}{4}$.

Use the data in the chart above. Find the experimental probability.

1. $P(\text{club})$ **2.** $P(\text{spade})$ **3.** $P(\text{diamond})$

Draw a card from a deck of 52 cards. Tally its suit in the table. Replace the card in the deck. Repeat the experiment 100 times. Write your experimental probabilities in the chart.

	Heart	Club	Diamond	Spade
Tally				
Total				
Experimental Probability				

Mathematics: Applications and Connections, Course 3

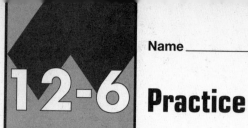

Name _____ Date _____

12-6 Practice

Experimental Probability

Use the graph at the right to complete Exercises 1 and 2.

1. Find the experimental probability of each outcome.
   a. $P(0 \text{ heads})$ **b.** $P(1 \text{ head})$

   c. $P(2 \text{ heads})$ **d.** $P(3 \text{ heads})$

2. Find the theoretical probability of each outcome.
   a. $P(0 \text{ heads})$ **b.** $P(1 \text{ head})$

   c. $P(2 \text{ heads})$ **d.** $P(3 \text{ heads})$

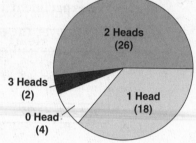

Three Pennies Tossed 50 Times

3. One dozen students each drop a brass tack six times from a height of six inches onto a level hard surface. They record the number of times the tack lands point-up. The table below lists their results.

Student	1	2	3	4	5	6	7	8	9	10	11	12
Point-up	2	3	3	4	3	6	5	3	5	4	3	4
Not point-up	4	3	3	2	3	0	1	3	1	2	3	2

   a. Find $P(\text{point-up})$ for each of the twelve students.

   b. If all the results are totaled, what is $P(\text{point-up})$?

   c. If $P(\text{point-up})$ and $P(\text{not point-up})$ have equal probabilities, what is the probability of the result obtained by student number 6?

4. Roll a die 50 times.
   a. Record the results.
   b. Based upon your record, what is the probability of a number greater than 4?

   c. Based upon your record, what is the probability of a number less than 3?

   d. The theoretical probabilities of parts **b** and **c** are equal. If your answers to **b** and **c** are not equal, does this mean that the die you rolled is not fair? Explain.

© Glencoe/McGraw-Hill   **98**   *Mathematics: Applications and Connections, Course 3*

12-7 Study Guide

Integration: Statistics
Using Sampling to Predict

Data gathered from a representative sample can be used to make predictions about a population.

Example   In a county survey of companies with between 500 and 1,000 employees, 82 said the number of employees had grown over the past year, 180 said the number of employees had remained the same, and 38 said the number of employees had decreased. If there are 12,000 companies with between 500 and 1,000 employees in the county, for how many might you expect that the number of employees grew over the past year?

Number of companies surveyed = 82 + 180 + 38 or 300

Solve a proportion to find the number of companies in the county that grew over the past year.

Sample companies that grew $\longrightarrow$ $\dfrac{82}{300} = \dfrac{x}{12,000}$ $\longleftarrow$ *Companies in the county that grew*
Total companies surveyed $\longrightarrow$ $\longleftarrow$ *Total companies in the county*

$$300x = 984,000$$
$$x = 3,280$$

From the survey, you might expect the number of companies in the county that grew over the past year to be 3,280.

Use the survey above to answer each question.

1. How many companies might you expect to have remained the same size over the past year?

2. How many companies might you expect to have decreased in size over the past year?

In a survey, 240 people said the city should build a new sports arena. 160 people said a new sports arena was too costly. If there are 500,000 voters in the city, predict each of the following.

3. number who will vote to build a new arena

4. number who will vote against building a new arena

Mathematics: Applications and Connections, Course 3

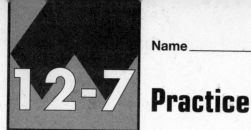

12-7 Practice

Integration: Statistics
Using Sampling to Predict

Use the survey of favorite pizza topping to answer each question.

Favorite Pizza Topping	
Cheese	85
Sausage	75
Mushroom	30
Other	50

1. What is the size of the sample?

2. What fraction chose sausage?

3. What fraction chose mushroom?

4. Seven hundred twenty pizzas a week are sold.
   a. How many cheese pizzas can be expected to be sold?
   b. How many pizzas from the "other" group can be expected to be sold?

The Plak-Attak Toothpaste Company surveys 800 dentists in New York State to see what type of toothpaste they recommend. Two hundred fifty-one dentists recommend the type of toothpaste that Plak-Attak makes. Which statements below are true?

5. More than half of all dentists surveyed prefer Plak-Attak type toothpaste!

6. More than one-third of all dentists surveyed prefer Plak-Attak type toothpaste!

7. More than one-fourth of all dentists surveyed prefer Plak-Attak type toothpaste!

8. More than 250 New York State dentists recommend Plak-Attak Toothpaste!

Book covers with the school insignia come in four colors: red, green, blue, and yellow. A survey of 80 students chosen at random was made to determine the student preferences.

9. There are 1,600 students in the school, and each student will buy an average of four book covers. About how many covers should the school store order?

10. Of the students surveyed, 40 chose red, 10 chose green, and 22 chose blue. How many chose yellow?

11. Based upon the survey, about how many book covers of each color should the store order?
   a. red   b. green   c. blue   d. yellow

13-1 **Study Guide**

Modeling Polynomials

A **monomial** is a number, a variable, or a product of a number and a variable. A **polynomial** is the sum or difference of two or more monomials. You can model monomials and polynomials using algebra tiles.

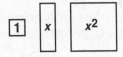

Examples **1** Model $-2x^2$.

2 Model $2x^2 - 3x + 4$.

Polynomial expressions can be evaluated by replacing variables with numbers and then finding the value of the expression.

Example 3 Evaluate $-x^2 + 2x - 3$, if $x = -5$.

$$-x^2 + 2x - 3 = -(-5)^2 + 2(-5) - 3 \qquad \textit{Replace x with } -5.$$
$$= -25 + (-10) - 3$$
$$= -38$$

Write a monomial or polynomial for each model.

1.

2.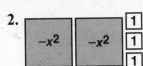

3.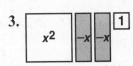

Model each monomial or polynomial.

4. $-3x^2$

5. $x^2 - x + 1$

6. $-2x^2 + 3x$

Evaluate each expression.

7. $2x + 1$, if $x = 3$

8. $x^2 + 4x$, if $x = -1$

9. $2x^2 - 3x + 5$, if $x = 2$

Mathematics: Applications and Connections, Course 3

13-1 Practice

Modeling Polynomials

Write a monomial or polynomial for each model.

1.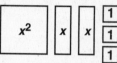

2.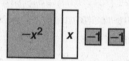

3.

4.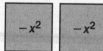

Model each monomial or polynomial using drawings or algebra tiles.

5. $x^2 - 3x$

6. $-2x^2 + 3x$

7. $4x + 1$

8. -6

Evaluate each expression.

9. $3x - 8$, if $x = 10$

10. $x^2 + 4x$, if $x = -4$

11. $x^2 + x + 3$, if $x = -2$

12. $3x^2 - 12$, if $x = 8$

13-2 Study Guide

Simplifying Polynomials

Each monomial in a polynomial is called a **term**. $3x^2$ and $2x^2$ are **like terms** because they have the same variable to the same power. You can simplify polynomials that have like terms. An expression that has no like terms is in **simplest form**.

Example   Simplify $3x^2 + x^2 + 4x - 3x + 2.$

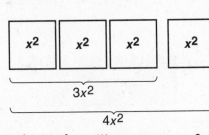

$3x^2$ and x^2 are like terms. $3x^2 + x^2 = 4x^2$
$4x$ and $-3x$ are like terms. $4x - 3x = x$

$3x^2 + x^2 + 4x - 3x + 2 = 4x^2 + x + 2$

Name the like terms in each list of terms.

1. $5m, -2m, m^2$

2. $7, 5v^2, -2, 3v$

3. $y^2, 7y, 8y^2, -2y$

Simplify each polynomial. Use drawings or algebra tiles if necessary.

4. $2x^2 - 5x - 2x^2 + x$

5. $2a - b + a - 3b$

6. $5c + 4 + 3 - 2c$

7. $-6t^2 - 3t + 4t^2 - t$

8. $2x^2 + 4x - 2x + 1$

9. $3x + 2y - y + x$

10. $-4c + 2c^2 - 1 + 3c$

11. $-2p + 3a - 4a + 6p$

Simplify each expression. Then evaluate if $x = 4$ and $y = -1.$

12. $x - 2y + 2x + y$

13. $4y - 2x + 3x - y$

14. $y + x - 3y - 3x$

13-2 Practice

Simplifying Polynomials

Name the like terms in each list of terms.

1. $3x, 2x, 4x^2, x$

2. $2a, 2b, 3a, 3b$

3. $5, 2x, 5y, 2$

4. $-3x^2, 2x^2, 3x, 4$

5. $2, x, y, 2x, 2y, 8, x^2$

6. $3x^2, 3x, 3$

Simplify each polynomial using the model.

7. $2a^2 - a - a^2 + 3a$

8. $3x - 2y + x - 2y + 2x + y$

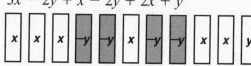

Simplify each polynomial. Use drawings or algebra tiles if necessary.

9. $4x + 3 + 2x + 4$

10. $-2x^2 + 3x - x^2 - x^2$

11. $6 + 3y^2 - 2 - y^2 + 5y$

12. $x^2 - x^2 - x^2 - x^2 - x$

13. $3x + 3y$

14. $2y + 1 - 2y + 1$

Simplify each expression. Then evaluate if a = 3 and b = −2.

15. $4a + 3b - a + 3b$

16. $a - b - b - a$

17. $b^2 - 4a - 2b^2$

18. $3x^2 + 2x - x^2 - 2x - 2x^2$

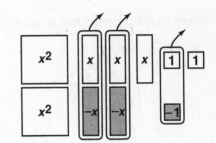

13-3 Study Guide

Adding Polynomials

To add polynomials, arrange like terms in columns. Then add.

Example   Find $(x^2 + 3x + 2) + (x^2 - 2x - 1)$.
Then evaluate the sum for $x = -3$.

$$\begin{array}{r} x^2 + 3x + 2 \\ +\ x^2 - 2x - 1 \\ \hline 2x^2 +\ x + 1 \end{array}$$

$$\begin{aligned} 2x^2 + x + 1 &= 2(-3)^2 + (-3) + 1 \quad \textit{Replace x with } -3. \\ &= 2(9) + (-3) + 1 \\ &= 18 - 3 + 1 \\ &= 16 \end{aligned}$$

Find each sum. Use drawings or algebra tiles if necessary.

1. $\begin{array}{r} 3x^2 + 2x + 5 \\ +\ 2x^2 -\ x + 3 \\ \hline \end{array}$

2. $\begin{array}{r} -6c^2 - 3c + 5 \\ +\ c^2 + 2c - 1 \\ \hline \end{array}$

3. $\begin{array}{r} -4a + 2b - 4c \\ +\ a - 3b - 2c \\ \hline \end{array}$

4. $(4x + 5y) + (-2x - y)$

5. $(x^2 + x + 1) + (x^2 - 2x + 3)$

6. $(5r + p) + (7r + 7p)$

7. $(6a^2 + 3a) + (2a^2 - 9a)$

8. $(5y^2 - 6y) + (-5y + 4)$

9. $(-2c^2 - 5) + 4c$

Find each sum. Then evaluate if x = -2 and y = 5.

10. $(4x + 2y) + (-2x + y)$

11. $(x + y - 6) + (-2x + y + 3)$

13-3 Practice

Name_____ Date_____

Adding Polynomials

Find each sum. Use drawings or algebra tiles if necessary.

1. $(2x + 3) + (x - 1)$

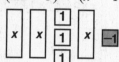

2. $(x^2 - x) + (2x - 2)$

3. $(x^2 + 2) + (-2x^2 + x)$

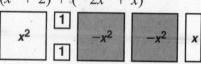

4. $(2x - 3) + (x^2 - 3)$

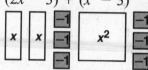

5. $\begin{array}{r} 3x^2 - 2x + 4 \\ + \quad\quad -8x - 3 \\ \hline \end{array}$

6. $\begin{array}{r} 4x^2 + x - 3 \\ + \quad x^2 + x - 5 \\ \hline \end{array}$

7. $\begin{array}{r} 2x^2 - \ x - 2 \\ + \ 3x^2 - 4x + 7 \\ \hline \end{array}$

8. $\begin{array}{r} 2w + 3y - \ z \\ + \ -2w - 4y - 5z \\ \hline \end{array}$

9. $(3x + 4y) + (2x + 3y)$

10. $(6r - 7s) + (2r - 8s)$

11. $(2a - 3) + (6a - 3)$

12. $(4x^2 + 3) + (-4x^2 + 8x - 3)$

Find each sum. Then evaluate if c = 5 and d = 8.

13. $(3c + d) + (c + 3d)$

14. $(6c - 3) + (-2c + d)$

15. $(4c + 3d - 6) + (2c - 3d - 6)$

16. $(5c + 2d + 3) + (-c - d - 3)$

Mathematics: Applications and Connections, Course 3

13-4 Study Guide

Subtracting Polynomials

You can subtract polynomials using algebra tiles.

Example 1   Find $(2x^2 + 3) - (-x^2 + 1)$.

Model $2x^2 + 3$.
To remove a negative x^2-tile,
first add a zero pair.
Remove the $-x^2$ tile.
Remove one 1-tile.

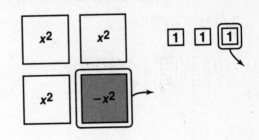

$$(2x^2 + 3) - (-x^2 + 1) = 3x^2 + 2$$

To subtract a polynomial, add the opposite of each term of the polynomial.

Example 2   Find $(2x^2 - 3x + 2) - (x^2 - 2x + 1)$.

$$\begin{array}{r} 2x^2 - 3x + 2 \\ - (x^2 - 2x + 1) \\ \hline \end{array} \qquad \begin{array}{r} 2x^2 - 3x + 2 \\ + (-x^2 + 2x - 1) \\ \hline x^2 - x + 1 \end{array}$$

The opposite of x^2 is $-x^2$.
The opposite of $2x$ is $-2x$.
The opposite of 1 is -1.

Find each difference. Use drawings or algebra tiles if necessary.

1. $(5t - 1) - (4t + 3)$

2. $(-3x - 2) - (2x + 1)$

3. $(4x^2 + 3) - (-x^2 - 5)$

4. $(-x^2 + 2x - 1) - (2x^2 + 3x + 2)$

5. $(6m + 2x) - (3m - 3x)$

6. $(7m^2 - 3m) - (-m^2 - 3m)$

7. $(-7x + 2y) - (-3x + 3y)$

8. $(4x^2 + 4x + 4) - (3x^2 - 3x - 3)$

*Mathematics: Applications
and Connections, Course 3*

13-4 Practice

Subtracting Polynomials

Find each difference. Use drawings or algebra tiles if necessary.

1. $(3x + 4) - (x + 2)$

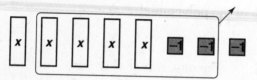

2. $(x^2 + 2x + 1) - (x + 1)$

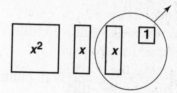

3. $(5x - 3) - (4x - 2)$

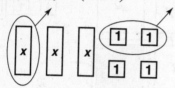

4. $(x^2 + x) - (2x + 1)$

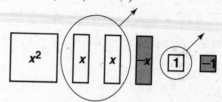

5. $\begin{array}{r} 2x + 8 \\ -\,(3x + 4) \end{array}$

6. $\begin{array}{r} 5x^2 + 2x - 3 \\ -\,(2x^2 + x - 6) \end{array}$

7. $(6s - 3) - (8s + 6)$

8. $(5x - 3) - (-5x - 3)$

9. $(3x^2 - 2x - 4) - (x^2 - 2x + 7)$

10. $(6a^2 - 2) - (a^2 - 3a)$

11. Find $(2x^2 - 3x - 4)$ minus $(4x^2 + 3x - 8)$.

12. What is $(3x^2 - 2xy + y^2)$ decreased by $(4x^2 - 3xy - y^2)$?

13-5 Study Guide

Multiplying Monomials and Polynomials

The products of powers property states that you can multiply powers that have the same base by adding their exponents: $a^m \cdot a^n = a^{m+n}$.

Examples **1** Find $4^3 \cdot 4$.

$$4^3 \cdot 4 = 4^{3+1}$$
$$= 4^4$$

2 Find $p^2 \cdot p^5$.

$$p^2 \cdot p^5 = p^{2+5}$$
$$= p^7$$

You can use the distributive property to multiply a polynomial by a monomial.

Example 3 Find $n(n-4)$.

Multiply each term inside the parentheses by n.

$$n(n-4) = n \cdot n - n \cdot 4$$
$$= n^2 - 4n$$

Find each product.

1. $3^3 \cdot 3$

2. $h^2 \cdot h^4$

3. $b^2 \cdot b^2$

4. $5(x+3)$

5. $x(x-2)$

6. $x(x+6)$

7. $3x(2x+1)$

8. $x(2x+3)$

9. $2x(x-1)$

Mathematics: Applications and Connections, Course 3

13-5 Practice

Multiplying Monomials and Polynomials

Find each product. Express the answer in exponential form.

1. $6 \cdot 6^5$

2. $k \cdot k$

3. $y^3 \cdot y^7$

Find each product.

4. $3(x + 1)$

3 $\begin{cases} \boxed{x} \ \boxed{1} \\ \boxed{x} \ \boxed{1} \\ \boxed{x} \ \boxed{1} \end{cases}$

$\underbrace{\hspace{2cm}}_{x + 1}$

5. $x(x + 2)$

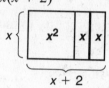

$\underbrace{\hspace{2cm}}_{x + 2}$

6. $3(x + 7)$

7. $4(a - 5)$

8. $3(2b - 4)$

9. $4(x + 3)$

10. $f(f + 9)$

11. $v(2v + 4)$

12. $2a(a - 1)$

13. $3x(2x - 4)$

14. $3(2b^2 - 1)$

15. $6h(2 - h)$

16. $14r(r^2 + 2)$

17. $9q(q^2 - q)$

18. $4z^2(z - 1)$

19. $5m^4(10 + m^2)$

20. Find the product of $6x$ and $3x - 4$.

13-6 Study Guide

Multiplying Binomials

A **binomial** is a polynomial with two terms. To find the product of two binomials, use algebra tiles or the distributive property.

Example   Find $(2x + 2)(x + 1)$.

Mark off a rectangle with width $(2x + 2)$ and length $(x + 1)$.

Using the marks as guides, fill in the rectangle with area tiles.

$(2x + 2)(x + 1) = 2x(x + 1) + 2(x + 1)$
$\qquad\qquad\qquad = 2x^2 + 2x + 2x + 2$
$\qquad\qquad\qquad = 2x^2 + 4x + 2$ *Simplify.*

Match each product with its corresponding model.

1. $(x + 2)(x + 3)$

2. $(2x + 1)(x + 2)$

3. $(x + 1)(2x + 3)$

4. $(x + 3)(x + 3)$

a.

b.

c.

d.

Find each product. Use algebra tiles or drawings if necessary.

5. $(x + 1)(x + 1)$

6. $(2x + 2)(x + 3)$

7. $(x + 5)(x + 3)$

8. $(x + 2)(x + 3)$

9. $(x + 5)(2x + 1)$

10. $(x + 2)(x + 2)$

13-6 Practice

Multiplying Binomials

Find each product.

1.

	$x + 3$		
x^2	x	x	x
x	1	1	1
x	1	1	1

$x + 2$

2.

	$2x + 4$					
x^2	x^2	x	x	x	x
x	x	1	1	1	1
x	x	1	1	1	1
x	x	1	1	1	1
x	x	1	1	1	1

$x + 4$

3. $(a + 3)(a + 5)$

4. $(3a + 2)(2a + 3)$

5. $(2x + 5)(x + 3)$

6. $(4y + 1)(4y + 2)$

Match each product with its corresponding model.

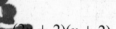

7. $(x + 3)(2x + 2)$

8. $(2x + 2)(x + 2)$

9. $(x + 1)(2x + 3)$

10. $(2x + 1)(x + 2)$

a.

x^2	x^2	x
x	x	1
x	x	1

b.

x^2	x^2	x	x
x	x	1	1
x	x	1	1

c.

x^2	x^2	x	x
x	x	1	1
x	x	1	1
x	x	1	1

d.

x^2	x^2	x	x	x
x	x	1	1	1

Find each product. Use drawings or algebra tiles if necessary.

11. $(4y + 5)(y + 2)$

12. $(x + 1)(x + 3)$

13. $(y + 3)(y + 1)$

14. $(3x + 2)(x + 4)$

15. $(3x + 2)(3x + 2)$

16. $(4x + 1)(2x + 2)$

13-7 Study Guide

Factoring Polynomials

To **factor** a polynomial means that you know the area of a rectangle and are asked to find the length and width.

Examples   **Factor each polynomial.**

1 $2x - 4$

Model the polynomial.

Try to form a rectangle with the tiles.

Write an expression for the length and width.

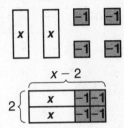

The rectangle has a width of 2 and a length of $x - 2$.
Therefore, $2x - 4 = 2(x - 2)$.

2 $x^2 + 3x + 2$

Model the polynomial.

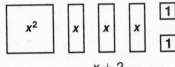

Form a rectangle.

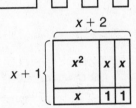

Write an expression.

The rectangle has a width of $x + 1$ and a length of $x + 2$.
Therefore, $x^2 + 3x + 2 = (x + 1)(x + 2)$.

If possible, factor each polynomial. Use drawings or algebra tiles if necessary.

1. $4y + 8$

2. $5x - 5$

3. $r^2 - 4r$

4. $6t^2 - 6$

5. $3m^2 + m$

6. $3x^2 + 3x$

7. $x^2 - 7x + 6$

8. $x^2 + 6x + 8$

9. $x^2 + 6x + 9$

Mathematics: Applications and Connections, Course 3

13-7 Practice

Factoring Polynomials

If possible, factor each polynomial.

1. $2x + 6$

| x | 1 | 1 | 1 |
| x | 1 | 1 | 1 |

2. $x^2 + 5x + 6$

x^2	x	x	x
x	1	1	1
x	1	1	1

3. $7x + 21$

4. $5x - 15$

5. $8x^2 - 8x$

6. $2x^2 + 4x$

7. $8x^2 + 2x$

8. $9x^2 + 6x$

9. $x^2 + 6x + 9$

10. $x^2 + 4x + 4$

11. $x^2 + 8x + 7$

12. $x^2 + 8x + 15$

13. $x^2 + 10x + 21$

14. $x^2 + 10x + 9$

15. $2x^2 + 7x + 3$

16. $2x^2 + 14x + 10$

17. $2x^2 + 3x + 1$

18. $2x^2 + 15x + 27$

19. $3x^2 + 5x + 2$

20. $4x^2 + 4x + 1$

Study Guide

The Tangent Ratio

The tangent ratio compares the measure of the leg opposite an angle with the measure of the leg adjacent to that angle.

If A is an acute angle of a right triangle, then

$$\tan A = \frac{\text{measure of the leg opposite } \angle A}{\text{measure of the leg adjacent to } \angle A}$$

Example 1 Use the tangent ratio to find the value of x.
From the diagram: $m\angle A = 15°$
adjacent leg $= x$ cm
opposite leg $= 24$ cm

$\tan 15° = \frac{24}{x}$ ← opposite leg
← adjacent leg

$(\tan 15°)(x) = 24$

$x = \dfrac{24}{\tan 15°}$

Use a calculator: 24 ÷ 15 TAN = 89.56921938
$x \approx 89.6$

Example 2 Find the measure of $\angle A$.

$\tan A = \frac{12}{17}$ ← opposite leg
← adjacent leg

Use a calculator:
12 ÷ 17 = 2nd [TAN⁻¹] 35.21759297
$m\angle A \approx 35°$

Complete each exercise using the information in the figure.
Find angle measures to the nearest degree.

1. $\tan A =$ _____

   $\tan B =$ _____

   $m\angle A =$ _____

   $m\angle B =$ _____

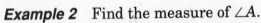

2. $\tan M =$ _____

   $\tan N =$ _____

   $m\angle M =$ _____

   $m\angle N =$ _____

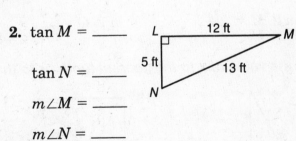

Find the value of x to the nearest tenth or degree.

3.

4.

5.
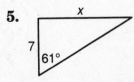

Mathematics: Applications and Connections, Course 3

Practice

The Tangent Ratio

Use the figures at the right for Exercises 1-8. Write the ratios in simplest form. Find angle measures to the nearest degree.

1. Find tan A.

2. Find $m \angle A$.

3. Find tan B.

4. Find $m \angle B$.

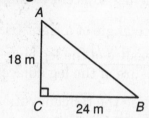

5. Find tan W.

6. Find $m \angle W$.

7. Find tan X.

8. Find $m \angle X$.

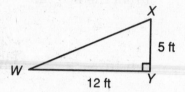

Complete each exercise using the information in the figure.
Find angle measures to the nearest degree.

9.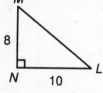

$\tan L = \underline{\ ?\ }$

$m \angle L = \underline{\ ?\ }$

$\tan M = \underline{\ ?\ }$

$m \angle M = \underline{\ ?\ }$

10.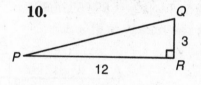

$\tan P = \underline{\ ?\ }$

$m \angle P = \underline{\ ?\ }$

$\tan Q = \underline{\ ?\ }$

$m \angle Q = \underline{\ ?\ }$

11.

$\tan F = \underline{\ ?\ }$

$m \angle F = \underline{\ ?\ }$

$\tan G = \underline{\ ?\ }$

$m \angle G = \underline{\ ?\ }$

Find the value of x to the nearest tenth or to the nearest degree.

12.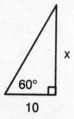

13.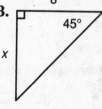

14.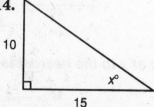

Study Guide

The Sine and Cosine Ratios

If an angle is an acute angle of a right triangle:

$$\sin A = \frac{\text{measure of the leg opposite } \angle A}{\text{measure of the hypotenuse}}$$

$$\cos A = \frac{\text{measure of the leg adjacent to } \angle A}{\text{measure of the hypotenuse}}$$

Example 1 Use the cosine ratio to find the value of x.
From the diagram: $m\angle A = 20°$
adjacent leg = 50 cm
hypotenuse = x cm

$\cos 20° = \frac{50}{x} \leftarrow$ adjacent leg
$\quad\quad\quad\quad \leftarrow$ hypotenuse

$(\cos 20°)(x) = 50$

$x = \dfrac{50}{\cos 20°}$

Use a calculator: 50 ÷ 20 [COS] = *53.20888862*
$x \approx 53$ cm

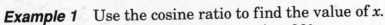

Example 2 Use the sine ratio to find the measure of $\angle A$.

$\sin A = \frac{12}{30} \leftarrow$ opposite leg
$\quad\quad\quad\quad \leftarrow$ hypotenuse

Use a calculator:
12 ÷ 30 =   [SIN⁻¹] *23.57817848*
$m\angle A \approx 24°$

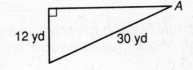

Complete each exercise using the information in the figure.
Find angle measures to the nearest degree.

1. $\sin A =$ _____

$\sin B =$ _____

$\cos A =$ _____

$\cos B =$ _____

$m\angle A =$ _____

$m\angle B =$ _____

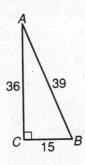

2. $\sin L =$ _____

$\sin M =$ _____

$\cos L =$ _____

$\cos M =$ _____

$m\angle L =$ _____

$m\angle M =$ _____

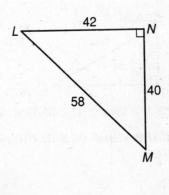

Find the value of x to the nearest tenth or to the nearest degree.

3.

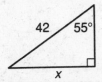

4.

5.

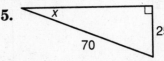

Mathematics: Applications and Connections, Course 3

Name_____ Date_____

Practice

The Sine and Cosine Ratios

Use the figures at the right for Exercises 1-12. Write the ratios in simplest form. Find angle measures to the nearest degree.

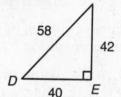

1. Find sin D.

2. Find cos D.

3. Find $m \angle D$.

4. Find sin F.

5. Find cos F.

6. Find $m \angle F$.

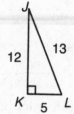

7. Find sin L.

8. Find cos L.

9. Find $m \angle L$.

10. Find sin J.

11. Find cos J.

12. Find $m \angle J$.

Complete each exercise using the information in the figure. Find angle measures to the nearest degree.

13.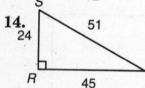

$\sin A = \underline{\ ?\ }$ $\cos A = \underline{\ ?\ }$ $m \angle A = \underline{\ ?\ }$

$\sin C = \underline{\ ?\ }$ $\cos C = \underline{\ ?\ }$ $m \angle C = \underline{\ ?\ }$

14.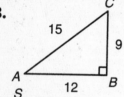

$\sin S = \underline{\ ?\ }$ $\cos S = \underline{\ ?\ }$ $m \angle S = \underline{\ ?\ }$

$\sin T = \underline{\ ?\ }$ $\cos T = \underline{\ ?\ }$ $m \angle T = \underline{\ ?\ }$

Find the value of x to the nearest tenth or to the nearest degree.

15.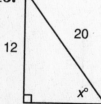

16.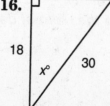

17.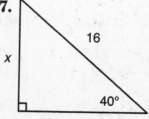

108

Mathematics: Applications and Connections, Course 3